FALSE MEMORIES

THE DECEPTION THAT SILENCED MILLIONS

Table of Contents

Acknowledgments

Thank you to every one of you who honored me by sharing your story in its entirety, many of you for the first time. Thank you for your patience when I contacted you again, wanting to make sure I got it right!

Thank you to:

Linda McEwen who has contributed so much to this book. For the past ten years she's saved me weeks of research time so that I could focus on assembling what I'd discovered into a book. When you see numbers, that's Linda's handiwork! Linda shared my vision to create a book that would empower survivors and the press to challenge the false memory proponents.

Lisa at the Prescott public library who always came through, however obscure the document, and to

Kirsten at the Washington State Bar News who emailed a pdf of "Repressed Memory Litigation" (which is not online) within 24 hours—at the start of the pandemic!

The Tri-City Herald for not jumping on the false memory train in the 1990s, and to SARC for keeping them informed.

The Leadership Council on Child Abuse and Interpersonal Violence whose members have kept me informed for two decades.

The conferences of the International Society for the Study of Trauma and Dissociation where I met those who study and treat the consequences of childhood trauma.

P. Anne Winter who continues to open up new avenues for thought, and to Sue and to Jennifer up the street who aren't afraid to ask questions. To filmmaker Mary Knight who helped me figure out the best approach for publishing this book.

Editors Mark Kramer and Wendy Call for "Telling True Stories" which I've read and re-read. And to screenwriter Brian McDonald with Seattle Writers who showed me that story makes sense not just in fiction, but in memoirs and nonfiction.

Harry Markopolis who laid out a road map for investigating a topic that everyone thinks they already know about.

My siblings who shared their stories and to retired Superior Court Judge Dennis Yule who heard us.

My son and daughter and their partners who are raising caring, thoughtful, resilient children.

Preface

When I sued my parents for damages in 1991, my community was supportive. After a month-long trial, the judge ruled in my favor in March 1994. I exited the courtroom as a successful plaintiff. I entered a community in denial. "Your memories are false," I was told. Hundreds of articles in the popular press quoting memory experts must have seemed like a crash course in memory. Nearly everyone was convinced my accusations and those of millions of others were false memories. I stopped talking about my childhood.

Following the trial, two of my parents' experts, sociologist Richard Ofshe, PhD, and memory researcher Elizabeth Loftus, PhD, challenged my accusations in published accounts. I challenged their claims, and so began my journey to discover the truth behind false memories.

Loftus published the lost-in-a-mall study in 1995. If memories of getting lost could be implanted in subjects, then supposedly, therapists could implant memories in clients of being sexually assaulted as a child by someone they loved and trusted. I wondered about the logic of that theory. Loftus testified during my lawsuit that she had dropped the first six subjects from her mall study. I wondered why she dropped those subjects.

Why hadn't the media challenged the "Therapists implanted those memories" claims of accused parents? I studied the tax returns from the parents' charity, the False Memory Syndrome Foundation. Parents had donated $7.75M to the foundation to fund their PR campaign. This helped me understand why their story had gone viral. Loftus had introduced the implanted memory story to the media.

I contacted the Society of Professional Journalists and learned that Loftus's PhD granted her an expert status the press would not challenge. Her PhD also gave her an expert platform to monetize false memories.

Sadly, the false memory story found a home in psychology textbooks. A generation of students has been told that memory is unreliable. Fortunately, the legal system sets a higher standard. Prosecutors have challenged Loftus's false memory claims. Her high-profile clients—ex-priest Paul Shanley, record producer Phil Spector, comedian Bill Cosby, movie producer Harvey Weinstein, real estate heir Robert Durst, and socialite Ghislaine Maxwell—were all found guilty.

Thirty years ago, accused parents and a PhD handed the media a too-good-to-be-true story. *False Memories: the Deception That Silenced Millions* tells the rest of the story.

Lynn Crook, MEd

PART 1

Becoming a False Memory Skeptic

Prologue

"UW Expert Challenges 'Repressed' Memories—Says Some Sexual Abuse May Not Be Real," the Associated Press announced on August 14, 1992.

Some sexual abuse may not be real? I'd sued my parents for damages the year before based on recovered memories of child sexual abuse. I was curious to see what this expert had to say.

Psychologist Elizabeth Loftus "believes false memories of abuse may be inadvertently suggested by therapists," the reporter said. This wasn't true in my case. My therapist had never suggested I was molested as a child.

"People are desperate for an explanation for their problems and feel this (past abuse) is the answer," the psychologist stated. This wasn't true in my case either. My problem was panic attacks. Joining my husband for a week-long business trip to San Francisco over Valentine's Day was the answer, not incest.

Surely a PhD wouldn't try to redefine a crime against children. She must be theorizing, I decided. Eighteen months later the psychologist was in the courtroom testifying for my parents. The judge ruled in my favor.

Following the trial, I reviewed my attorney's deposition of the psychologist and something caught my attention. Six subjects had completed the lost in a mall study. The six subjects were dropped, she reported. I decided to find out why. What I discovered led to more questions over the next decade, and those answers led to this book.

Chapter 1

What We Tell Ourselves

We are trusting as long as he isn't poor and toothless and/
or of a different ethnic group, as long as he looks like
us and talks like us—most certainly if he's a priest or
pediatrician or teacher.

—Anna Salter, *Predators—Pedophiles, Rapists and*
Other Sex Offenders, **2003**

1988

My community had made up its mind about child molesters. "They should all be strung up by dawn," I was told repeatedly during my first few months as an agency crisis counselor and community educator. I soon learned what they really believed.

The local *Tri-City Herald* reported the arrest of a popular middle school teacher accused of showing child porn to two boys. Detectives found the porn on the teacher's computer and he was arrested. "Good," I thought. "The school will support those boys."

I stopped by the middle school one morning to drop off some flyers. I introduced myself to the school secretary, handed her a flyer and asked, "Okay if I put these on the display table?"

She glanced at the flyer and said, "Isn't it just terrible the way those boys are trying to ruin that nice teacher's reputation?

Shocked, I didn't respond. I placed the flyers on the table, waved, and headed out to my car. That "nice" teacher didn't have to worry about being strung up by dawn, I realized.

The *Herald* followed up with the story of a popular grade school teacher in a nearby small town. He was charged with molesting one of his students. The townspeople held a bake sale to raise money for his legal expenses. The community was shunning the girl and her mother. I wondered if any of the students watching this drama play out at their school had told themselves, "They won't believe me either."

My community wasn't "stringing them up by dawn." They were supporting the ones they knew. Child molesters weren't out there waiting in cars or standing in alleys. They were in families and schools with the children.

Just Trying to Help

> It is very tempting to take the side of the perpetrator. All the perpetrator asks is that the bystander do nothing. He appeals to the universal desire to see, hear and speak no evil. The victim, on the contrary, asks the bystander to share the burden of pain. The victim demands action, engagement and remembering.

—Judith Herman, *Trauma and Recovery*

Clients reported what they were hearing from their friends and family members who were "Just trying to help." This advice sounded more like they were trying to silence our clients. How would audiences respond if they heard those comments coming from me, I wondered. I prepared a handout and read the "Just trying to help" comments aloud to audiences with all the drama I could muster. I was relieved to hear them laugh. I hoped that laughter might resolve some of their ambivalence towards perpetrators.

Just Trying to Help	Helpful Responses
Isn't it about time you got over this?[1]	*Listen.*
This will ruin his reputation.	*I'm glad you could tell me. Thank you.*
He couldn't help it.	
Ah well, boys will be boys.	
Forgive him and get on with your life.	
He never did that to me.	
This won't bring back your childhood.	
This will just kill your _____.	
I don't believe in airing dirty linen.	
Was he molested?	
This is a family/personal matter.	
Children get over this.	
Are you sure?	

Chapter 2

Back to the Memories

Our clients inspired me with their courage. The agency staff was knowledgeable and compassionate. The detectives who interviewed our clients were kind and compassionate. There was just one problem. The agency director was a faultfinding, taciturn, older woman with a hands-on management style. She reminded me of my father, but I didn't know why.

As the weeks passed, I experienced occasional moments of shaky panic at work. I couldn't breathe. A neurologist found no physical cause for the panic attacks and referred me to a therapist.

After three sessions with Eric, a therapist I knew from the agency, my anxiety at work continued. I just needed a vacation, I decided. I joined my husband for a week-long business trip to San Francisco over Valentine's Day in 1989.

"I'm fine," I told Eric, smiling contentedly as we began our fourth session. "No panic attacks in California."

"I'm glad to hear that," he said, adding, "So tell me about your family."

"My family is great," I said in a tone that I still recall as sounding oddly flat. "My father is a doctor. My mother is a stay-at-home mom with a nursing degree. She's an artist. She says Dad reminds her of Gary Cooper, tall and handsome, a man of few words. He plays golf. I'm the oldest of six." I added, "We were well-behaved; we did well in school."

Finding little else to say, I told Eric what I thought, at that moment, was just a bit of family trivia.[2] "When I was a teenager, my father made me stop having periods." And with those words, at age 45, the wall of silence that I had so painstakingly constructed as a child wobbled ever so slightly.

Eric responded as anyone might have. He asked, "How did your father make you stop having periods?"

I froze, panicked. I cried out silently, "No, no it wasn't that! Did he think my father . . ." I stopped that thought. I looked over at the door. I desperately wanted to stand up, walk over to the door, turn the knob, open the door and go home. But I couldn't move.

I took a deep breath. I had to appear calm so Eric wouldn't think there was something wrong with me. Then I told him the rest of the story. My mother made an appointment with their gynecologist friend. "He said I wasn't pregnant," I told Eric, "but I knew that." I continued. "The doctor told me, 'Sometimes periods stop because of worries.' When he said 'worries,' I knew what the problem was. My father's criticism of my hair, my table manners, my weight, my laziness. I couldn't do anything right."

I told Eric what I told my mother on the drive home, "I don't think Dad loves me very much."

"That's just the way he is," she assured me. "He has a hard time showing his feelings."

"The next day Dad took me aside and told me that he loved me. He looked about as uncomfortable as I felt during our brief conversation," I said. "After that, everything was fine."

Back at home on that dark February evening, I stood at the kitchen sink rinsing the dinner dishes as the night rain ran down the window. The sound of the water rushing from the faucet seemed to grow louder as I seemed to be standing in a shower stall, my father towering over me, as he grabbed my small hand and pressed it to a body part of his that I had no name for.

I froze. "No!" But I knew what this was. A flashback. I'd described this phenomenon in presentations. A long-buried memory had delivered itself like a package FedEx'd from my childhood.

"Interesting," I told myself again and again over the next few days. "I'm just fine," I assured myself. "Okay, so now I know what a flashback is. Great. No big deal. It only happened once." Then I recalled another incident. Dismayed, I told myself, "Well maybe it happened twice." Then I remembered more.

Chapter 3

The Power of Telling

I still hadn't told a soul what had triggered everything.
Some part of me was still too worried about what people
would think of me. I guess I was afraid that they would
perceive me as weak, or damaged, or somehow at fault
for what had happened to me in that apartment when I
was seven years old.

—Keyon Dooling, *Running from a Ghost*, 2018

Unless you talk about it, unless it gets out there, unless you
know there are people that care about you regardless of what
has happened to you, unless you know that, it's hard to get
to the place where you feel comfortable not only talking
about that, but talking about what it's made you into."[3]

**—R.A. Dickey, *Wherever I Wind Up—My Quest for Truth,
Authenticity and the Perfect Knuckleball***

One evening after our teenage daughter and son had gone to bed, I
decided the time had come to tell my husband. I was nervous. I felt
ashamed and disgusted by what I was remembering. I was afraid Bob
would be so repelled by what I'd done that he would leave me. But
I had to know. I kept it brief. "Bob, I need to tell you something," I
quickly described the shower incident. I assured him, "Don't worry.
I'll take care of this. "You don't have to worry about me." He didn't

turn away. Instead, I saw only tenderness in his eyes as he reached out to hold me in his arms.

We told our daughter and son. We discussed how this might impact their relationship with their grandparents who lived in the next town.

Over the next several weeks, I told four of my five younger siblings what I'd remembered. They expressed no shock. Instead, they shared similar experiences, a vague memory, an always-remembered memory, a recovered memory, and boundary violations.

I had one more sibling left to tell when I made some mistakes. My mother told me my sister and her husband were heading for Hawaii and leaving their two young children with my parents. I didn't call my sister and tell her what I had remembered. Instead, I asked my mother for advice. Should I tell my sister about Dad? My brother-in-law really needed this trip, my mother said. She would keep an eye on the kids. I was working at the agency and told her I would drop by. I kept putting off the visit because I couldn't bear to be around my father. When they returned, I couldn't bear to call my sister because I'd realized it would be my fault if dad molested them. My mother called to say the kids were checked by their doctor and they were fine. Relieved, I called my sister to tell her how glad I was to hear they were okay. During that phone call I thought to myself, "If he molested them, I'd have evidence." I felt awful for that thought and apologized to my sister in tears.

I sent a letter to my father's younger brother in Seattle telling him what I'd remembered. Maybe I might learn more. He told me about the time he and my aunt visited us in Kennewick. "After dinner," he said, "Bruce took you all off to bed. He never came back. I asked Lucille where he was. 'The girls have nightmares,' your mother said. He was pretty open about what he was doing to you." My uncle said my father was awkward around women. He had a hard time getting dates.

Before False Memories

> Instead of the negative response I feared, I have been met
> with overwhelming love and affirmation.
>
> **—Danielle Bostick, Psychotherapist, "'I feel whole.' After
> 30 years, a woman confronts her abuser—and herself,"**
> ***Washington Post*, 2014**

I recalled in early 1989, three years before the false memory campaign began. As a child, I was able to "archive" the incidents, to bury them so I wouldn't have to think about the awful stuff. My memory had kept me safe. Then, like for so many, my memory became my teacher when I was better able to deal with the shame, the betrayal and the feelings of powerlessness.

Each time I told a friend I was molested by my father, I shook with anxiety. I tried to hide it by holding my arms close to my body. I didn't feel especially courageous. I knew I had to do this for myself. Friends responded with compassion making my anxiety and shame a little easier to bear each time I told. *The Courage to Heal* co-author Laura Davis describes this process. "There's an incredible feeling of relief that the secret is out, and the person can move through the feelings of shame and isolation to start the healing process."[4]

I still didn't want to believe my father did these embarrassing things to me. A few months into therapy Eric, asked, "What would it mean to you if you were to decide that your memories are false?"

Great question, I thought. I told him, "When I remember, I feel sickened by the awfulness of what he did. When I tell you what I've remembered, it's like vomiting it back up, it's like getting it out of me for good." I added, "You help me to see how what happened to me as a child has impacted my life. Deciding my memories are false would be like swallowing that awful stuff back down again. I can't do that."

Telling Her

> Mothers or mother substitutes were at least
> passively involved in nearly half (46%) of all in-
> scope sexual abuse cases.
>
> **—*National Survey of the Incidence and Severity of
> Child Abuse and Neglect*, 1981, p. 32**[5]

Based on my experience as a mother of two, I knew that mothers can be trusted to protect their children. Years earlier we had left our young children with my parents when we attended an out-of-state funeral.[6] Thinking back, I couldn't recall any signs suggesting Dad molested them when we returned. With that in mind, I invited my mother for lunch. After the waitress delivered our orders I announced, "Mom, I have something to tell you." I quickly described a few of the incidents I'd remembered.

She expressed no shock. Instead, she paused for a moment and responded, "I believe you." She continued speaking and for the first time, I was able to hear her without the filter I must have used since childhood to screen out the illogic and craziness. She explained what she seemed to think were the duties of a thrifty wife. "I put you in the bathtub with him," she explained, "so we could save on water. I put you in bed with him so he could keep you warm and we could save on electricity." A baby waking up during the night meant "I had to wake up one of you to keep your dad company in bed." She told me about the time she went into their bedroom and Dad jumped out of bed with an erection. She stood next to the bed, scolding me for being too old to be in bed with my father. A few weeks later, she cleared out the storage room. "This is your new bedroom," she announced. I painted the cement block walls a pale aqua.

"Did he ever put it in," she asked.

I was pretty sure she meant penile penetration. "No," I told her. She smiled, perhaps in relief.[7]

She had known, I realized. But she didn't let herself know. She had made it easy for him.

Telling Him

> What if you found the perfect crime, one that you could commit repeatedly and never get caught? This crime enables your addiction, allowing you to do exactly what you prefer most. You spend your whole life perfecting your image to ensure that others will trust you. You have a position of power where the community respects and believes you.

—**Lisa Monaco Gonzales,** *San Diego Union-Tribune,* **2012**

My father bullied us into silence as children, confident he would never be reported. Media coverage of child sexual abuse in the 1980s may have come as a shock to him. Children were supposed to forget about things like that.

I invited my father to what was called a "confrontation." I'd discussed this session in detail with Eric. My father would be the last family member to learn what I'd remembered. I didn't expect him to confess. I knew by then that only five percent confess.

Dad opened the door to Eric's office and stood there silently, looking stiff and stern. I quickly looked down at my notes. "Come in, Dr. M.," Eric said, gesturing to the empty chair in the far corner of the office. Dad crossed the room and eased his lanky body down into the chair. He leaned back, folded his arms across his chest, and looked around at us expectantly. Eric thanked him for joining us and said, "Lynn has something she wants to tell you." Eric turned to me.

I took a deep breath. I looked at my father, and said, "Here's what I remember that you did to me when I was a child." I read aloud the list of twelve incidents I'd remembered by then. After each incident, I glanced over at him to see his reaction. He appeared calm, casually interested. He smiled slightly after I read the seventh incident and I thought, "He remembers that one."

I finished the list, paused, and turned to look at him. "I don't remember any of that," he said in a calm voice.

I continued, describing the consequences I'd experienced—the panic attacks; my anxiety around horses, dogs, and tall men; the bouts of depression; the chronic stomach and vaginal problems; my inability to recall any everyday stories that happened inside our home. I paused, then asked, "Would you pay for my therapy?"

He glanced away, looking thoughtful. Then he looked at Eric and said, "Yes, I'll pay for the therapy, but I don't remember any of it." I smiled with relief. I felt a sense of calm that I hadn't felt in a long time. It was over. My father was willing to take responsibility for the damage he had caused. He hadn't apologized. But I believed that he might one day acknowledge what he had done as our relationship began to improve—as it surely would now.

"He didn't seem surprised," Eric pointed out after Dad left.

My mother called a few days later. "Bruce," she said in a stern voice, "talked to an attorney. Paying for your therapy could make him liable in a lawsuit. So," she said, "Bruce won't pay for your therapy." She hung up. We never spoke again.

Tolerating Them

As a child, I didn't wonder why my father did this. He made it seem normal, as if it were just something fathers do that we aren't supposed to talk about. As an adult, I finally accepted that I would never know why unless he told me. And if he told me, it wouldn't make sense.

As a child, I hoped my mother would stop him. As an adult, I wondered why my mother tolerated a husband who committed crimes against her six children. Perhaps he assured her as a physician he could be trusted not to harm us. Perhaps she believed him.[8] Or perhaps they never spoke of it at all.

Perhaps she tolerated the abuse because his income as a general practitioner provided her with a middle-class life, a step up from her childhood. Since she had benefitted from allowing him to have sexual contact with her children, she had trafficked her children. I'd like to think that had she been able to see herself in this light, she would have stopped him.

Chapter 4

The Safety of Forgetting

In order to escape accountability for his crimes,
the perpetrator does everything in his power
to promote forgetting.

—Judith Lewis Herman, *Trauma and Recovery:*
The Aftermath of Violence—From Domestic Abuse
to Political Terror, **1994**

A child molested by a stranger can run home for help and
comfort. A victim of incest cannot.

—Heidi Vanderbilt, "Incest, A Chilling Report,"
Lears Magazine, **February 1992**

The Logic of Repression

Silencing young victims, insisting they "forget," makes sense for both
the molester and the child. The molester doesn't have to worry about
being reported.[9] The child doesn't have to think about the awfulness
of what he does. I could shut off my feelings of despair, disgust and
fear.

Child molesters bully their young victims into silence—they may
threaten to kill the family pet, or harm a younger sibling, or convince
the child they will go to hell, etc. I was perhaps 6-years-old when
I told someone. My parents were informed. Dad sat me down and

scolded me. If I ever told family secrets again, he said, people would think I was crazy. I would have to leave the family and go live in the crazy house (Eastern State Hospital) at Medical Lake. He pointed out the facility on a family trip to Spokane. I didn't want to leave my family. I didn't want to go to the crazy house.

"Children forget this sort of thing," he told me. "Whenever you think about it," he said, "tell yourself, 'Forget it.'" I followed his instructions. At age 6, I was learning many new skills. "Forget it" was just another skill.

After I recalled, I dreamed about a little Gothic church atop a hill with no other buildings in sight. The church grounds were bare and uneven as if they had been dug up. For me, that dream symbolized where I'd buried the memories as a child—in an abandoned, sacred place.

The "forget it" skill followed me into adulthood. At a family gathering shortly before I recalled, my husband witnessed my body become rigid as Dad stood behind me. Curious, my husband asked me about this after everyone left. I told him I remembered this as if I were seeing it from across the room as my father grabbed my buttock and I froze, I couldn't move.

The Safety of Repression

Some say there is no evidence a child can repress or dissociate frightening incidents, and then accurately remember the incident as an adult. Take the example of a high school reunion, they say. We didn't repress those memories, we just didn't think about them. Yet repression, for some children, is a matter of survival. It's a safe place. Survivors and experts describe this phenomenon.

In *Blind to Betrayal*, Jennifer Freyd and Pamela Birrell ask readers to imagine a young boy who gets molested by his father at night. "When his father walks into the room while the boy is eating breakfast, if a little thought starts to form in the boy's mind about the molestation . . . he can focus his attention on something else in the room" (pp. 88-89).

Filmmaker Mary Knight says, "There is no job as demanding as surviving an abusive childhood. Delayed recall for a child is like taking a vacation from the fear, horror, and shame of the abuse."[10]

Psychiatrist Heather Hall explains, "When trapped and alone in a painful environment, each child uses their own natural ability to dissociate and detach as the primary coping tool."[11]

Child psychologist Joyanna Silberg describes repression as an ongoing process over time engaging specific parts of the brain that inhibit memory (p. 98).[12]

Danielle Bostick was molested by her swim coach. She describes how, as a child, she was "Frantically burying memory fragments of the trauma and constructing an alternate reality."[13]

Senior Political Reporter Andrea Grimes explains, "I built—like, really, purposefully built—delicate, intricate, elaborate mind-paths, each of which navigated away from and around one thing: my abuse. I did it consciously at first, and then as I became older, my brain seemed to do it for me, automatically."[14]

Marilyn Van Derbur describes how one part of her stayed in the room to take what she had to take, and the other part went out and became successful. Accepting the part who stayed behind required several years of therapy and medical treatment.[15]

The Power of Remembering

> There is no greater agony than bearing an
> untold story inside you.

—Maya Angelou, *I Know Why the Caged Bird Sings*

Remembering the traumatic incidents of my childhood has been like walking along a beach during a storm. Giant, powerful memories pound in and pull back, leaving behind confusing, disgusting, shameful debris from other times and places. My fears of horses, dogs and tall men had been dictated by a reality I didn't remember. What I remembered showed me I had good reasons to be fearful as a child. Therapy showed me I could leave those fears behind.

One of the most painful incidents I recalled did not involve any physical contact. A younger sister and I were in bed with Dad one morning when I heard our mother's footsteps coming down the hall. The bedroom door was open. "Finally," I thought, "she'll see what he's doing and make him stop." I kept my eyes on the doorway. I watched as she paused at the door, carrying the baby in her arms. We made eye contact for a moment. Then she turned away and continued down the hall. I was on my own.

I have no memory of the peripheral details of that incident. I don't remember what was happening in the bed or what my mother was wearing. I remember only the core of that incident—the footsteps, the eye contact, the turning away, and the realization that I would have to figure this out for myself.

Chapter 5

The Road to Justice

Standing in the checkout line at the local Safeway grocery store one morning in 1991, a *People Magazine* cover caught my attention. The bold, white text announced *A STORY OF INCEST—MISS AMERICA'S TRIUMPH OVER SHAME. It began at age 5. Now Marilyn Van Derbur tells of her shocking 13-year ordeal of sexual abuse by her millionaire father. In 'The Darkest Secret' Former Miss America Marilyn Van Derbur Bravely Shares Her Difficult Past. Behind the Facade of a 'Perfect' Family, Her Father Committed An Unspeakable Crime: Incest.*

A magazine actually let someone say something like that about her father? Shocked, I tossed a copy into the grocery cart, made my way through the checkout line, and hurried out to the car. On page 88, there it was, *The Darkest Secret—Behind the façade of a "perfect" family, the unspeakable crime: incest, by Marilyn Van Derbur Atler.* The byline said "Marilyn Van Derber Atler." *People Magazine* let her tell her own story.

On a warm September afternoon in 1991, I entered the Benton County Justice Center in Kennewick and told the clerk, "I want to file a lawsuit." She handed me the forms, and I filled in the information that would begin the process of holding my parents accountable for the crimes they committed against me as a child. I was aware of some of the challenges I would face. The community would find out about my shameful, embarrassing childhood. My parents would be angry about being outted like this. Family members might not agree with my decision, they might shun me. I might hear negative comments from my father's former patients, his doctor friends, and his golfing buddies. My mother's church friends would surely stand by her.

I knew that holding a child molester accountable for his crime and the damage he had caused was the right thing for me to do. I admired the courage of the clients who reported the offender to authorities and testified in court. I could do no less. I was on a journey to find justice, a journey that began on a February evening in 1989 as I stood at the kitchen sink. I wasn't certain what I would learn on this journey. I believed I had what I needed to see this journey through to its end. I had a kind, wise husband. My case was corroborated with a variety of evidence. In Barbara Jo Levy I had an experienced, knowledgeable and wise attorney.

I returned home that afternoon and found the September 1991 issue of *Columns*, the University of Washington (UW) alum magazine in my mailbox. "Buried Memories," featured UW psychology professor Elizabeth Loftus and Lucy Berliner, the research director at the Harborview Sexual Assault Center. Repressed memories are potentially "the topic of the decade" Loftus suggested. My parents were UW alums. They would read this article.[16] The campaign to silence the claims of adults molested as children had begun.

A front-page headline in the local *Tri-City Herald* on Sunday, October 20, 1991, announced, "Woman accuses doctor father in sex abuse suit." *For 45 years, Lynn Crook feared her father, a long-time Kennewick doctor, but she says she didn't know why. She says she felt awkward around him and wondered why she remembered nothing about her family life while growing up in the Tri-Cities. . . .*

"We don't feel that they're justified," said Dr. M., 82. "I would say that none of them happened."

She expects to be criticized by people who will not understand her actions. Some may accuse her of trying to destroy her parents or of being a vengeful daughter.

"Part of me is very scared," she admitted. "But I'm standing up saying to offenders everywhere to watch out because someday one of their victims may do the same to them."

I received over 70 letters from Tri-City residents supporting my decision to hold my parents accountable. No one expressed any surprise. I heard reports about my father. Two women, a family member and a co-worker said he had made demeaning remarks to them when they were hospital patients. A hospital nurse telephoned and said he verbally abused the hospital nurses. They sometimes had to deliver his patients' babies themselves, she said. They called him, but he wouldn't show up. One mother said he didn't use a numbing agent before stitching up the laceration on her young son's hand. Her son had to learn to be a man, my father told her. A friend told me she was married, pregnant and a high school senior when she made an appointment with my father. She said she experienced a sharp pain during the pelvic exam. She miscarried hours later. A Hospice volunteer told me he was one of the two least-respected physicians in the city. These reports saddened me, but they did not surprise me.

My father had bullied me into silence as a child. He convinced me that people would think I was crazy if I told anyone. When the Herald reported my lawsuit in 1991, I learned that my parents were telling friends and family members, "Lynn is crazy, menopausal, in league with the devil, confused, a pathological liar."

The Implanted Memory Response

The local Tri-City Herald followed a year later with an Associated Press (AP) headline, "UW Expert Challenges `Repressed' Memories—Says Some Sexual Abuse May Not Be Real."[17]

I reviewed the article to see if it applied to my case. "Some repressed memories of sexual abuse may be false, although they doubtless are believed by those who report them, University of Washington psychologist Elizabeth Loftus says." The psychologist's "may be false" description didn't apply to my case. My accusations were corroborated by family members.

The expert's suggestion that the memories were "inadvertently suggested by therapists" didn't apply to my case either. My therapist had never suggested I was molested.

"People are desperate for an explanation for their problems and feel this (past abuse) is the answer." My problem was panic attacks. Joining my husband for a week-long business trip to San Francisco and dining at wonderful restaurants was the answer, not incest.

The psychologist's claims must apply to other cases, I decided, because they didn't apply to mine. I became a false memory skeptic that day. I didn't believe false memory claims, I analyzed them.

Eighteen months later, the expert quoted in the article was in the Benton County courthouse testifying for my parents at $350 per hour.

By the time Crook v. M. went to trial in February 1994, the public had been hearing for two years that abuse accusations like mine are false memories. My attorney had ruled out a jury trial, thinking I might not receive a fair hearing. We would leave it up to Judge Dennis Yule.

February 1994: *Lynn Crook v. Bruce and Lucile M.*, Benton County, Washington

Seated in the courtroom with my attorney on the first day of the trial, I glanced across the aisle at my parents. They looked away. We would spend the month of February in the courtroom without exchanging a word.

My four sisters testified, describing incidents of Dad's sexual abuse and boundary violations. My husband testified about the incident he had witnessed when my father grabbed my buttock. My two therapists testified as well as the three experts who interviewed me— psychologist Shirley Feldman-Summers and sociologist Jon Conte who testified for me—and Dr. Harris who testified for my parents. Psychologist Elizabeth Loftus and sociologist Richard Ofshe, who did not interview me, testified for my parents. A local veterinarian testified for my parents.

My parents had been the all-powerful adults throughout my childhood. They had violated boundaries and bullied me into silence. Under cross-examination, my father struggled to explain why he testified in his deposition that it wasn't sexual abuse if a father made his daughter touch his penis. He didn't think it was abuse at the time, he explained, but he had since learned it was.

My mother struggled to explain a letter she had written to one of my sisters. Judge Yule stated in his decision, "The tenor of the letter in its entirety does not seem to me to be consistent with a firm belief in Dr. M.'s innocence." A colleague from the agency overheard her tell Dad, "We wouldn't be here if I hadn't taken bed rest when I was pregnant with her." They wouldn't have been there if she'd stopped him, I wanted to tell her.

My parents appeared uneasy and confused on the witness stand, yet very insistent, as they responded to my attorney's questions. I was embarrassed for them. I was relieved for them that their friends weren't in the courtroom watching them struggle to appear calm while my attorney publicly confronted them. Here, they couldn't bully my attorney into silence. As I watched their discomfort and embarrassment, the shame I had carried for so many years returned to where it belonged—with my parents.

I told my attorney afterward that I wished everyone who was molested as a child could see their offender(s) confronted like this.

The False Memory Experts

Sociology professor Richard Ofshe entered the courtroom midway during the trial to testify for my parents. My mother appeared awestruck as she approached this elegantly dressed, false memory celebrity to introduce herself. I overheard him tell her, "I can't promise I'll win this for you."

A second false memory celebrity, psychology professor Elizabeth Loftus, arrived on another morning wearing a grey, pinstripe suit over a wrinkled, white blouse. Half a dozen local attorneys sat at the rear of the courtroom observing her testimony. During the lunch break, I noticed my parents were sitting by themselves in the courthouse cafeteria while Loftus shared a table with their attorney across the room.

Loftus returned to the courthouse several months later to testify for another defendant. I was told she stopped by Judge Yule's office and invited him to meet with her. She said she wanted to discuss a decision he'd made that she didn't agree with. He declined her invitation.

My Testimony

My attorney called me up to testify. As I responded to my attorney's questions, I could feel Judge Yule's cool gaze as he considered my testimony. I spoke of the experiences I had archived as a child so that no one would know what Dad did to us. As he said he might, my husband left the courtroom when my attorney asked me about the long-term consequences of the abuse—the depressive episodes, the panic attacks, my sexual behavior, the shame of having nothing to say when friends talked about their families, my always-bandaged fingers, my fear of appearing crazy, my fear of standing up for myself. Then my parents' attorney stood to begin his cross-examination. I answered him truthfully. I answered only the questions he asked. Then it was over. Now, it was up to the judge.

The Verdict

On March 4, 1994, following four weeks of testimony, we were back in the courtroom. My hopes went up, then down, as Judge Yule read his decision to the court. Finally he concluded, "Accordingly, in this case, the plaintiff is granted judgment in the amount of $149,580. That is the Court's decision, Counsel. I will sign the appropriate judgment upon presentation. Court will be in recess."

We won! Overcome with relief and happiness, I turned to my husband and hugged this wonderful man who had stood by me, and encouraged me to stand up for myself. I hugged my attorney whose examination of my family members had revealed stories I'd never known. I thanked my friends and the agency volunteers who attended the trial.

"Daughter wins sex abuse case against parents—Judge awards $149,580 in damages," the *Herald* announced. There was once a time when suing was an act of faith for me, like spitting in the eyes of all the child molesters out there, challenging them, "This could happen to you one day so you'd better stop molesting that child." In the end, I held my parents accountable for what my father did, and for what my mother didn't do. I did this for me and for the terrified, silent child that I was. I have never regretted that decision.

Judge Yule's decision is online at http://blogs.brown.edu/recoveredmemory/files/2010/06/Crook-Redacted.pdf

My mother died in 1995, my father in 2000.

Chapter 6

Who Tells Our Story?

My community was supportive when I sued my parents in 1991. When I left the courtroom in 1994 after proving my case in court, the public had a new story. They had been inundated with hundreds of false memory articles. When I talked about my case I was told, "I read about those false memories. You saw a therapist? How are your parents doing?"

"But I won the case, my memories are corroborated," I insisted. It made no difference. They were convinced my memories were false. I'd read some of those same articles, I'd watched a few talk shows. I questioned false memory claims. I assumed everyone would do the same.

False memories were news in the 1990s. Few knew the headlines were the result of an extremely successful media campaign, coordinated and funded by parents accused of committing crimes against their children. False memory claims made up 85% of the media coverage on sexual assault. [18] I stopped speaking about my childhood. I wondered how many thousands of others were silenced. How were they coping without the compassionate support I'd received before the campaign began?

Perhaps the parents' campaign made reporters feel as if they were doing a Good Thing. They were informing the public of the Truth about adults' accusations. They were false. The parents' campaign resolved any ambivalence the media might have had about accused parents. They were falsely accused.

I wondered why the reporters didn't fact-check the claims of the parents' experts they quoted. I called the Society of Professional Journalists. I learned that reporters don't challenge PhDs. They assume that PhDs are experts so their statements must be accurate. A journalist's duty, I learned, is to interview individuals from both sides of an issue, not fact-check their statements.

A brief item appeared in *USA Today: KENNEWICK—A judge awarded $150,000 to Lynn Crook, 50, who says her parents sexually abused her as a child. Her parents offered no comment.* Producers from *Frontline* and the *Montel Williams Show* called and asked if I would tell my story. "Of course," I told them, assuming they were interested in my story. They asked for my parents' phone number. I never heard back. I will be forever grateful to my parents for not appearing on those programs. My story of an adult molested as a child who sought justice in the courtroom was not the story *Frontline* or Montel Williams wanted to tell.

A friend who attended the trial invited me to discuss my experience at the luncheon meeting of her local service group. I'd presented to this group three years earlier in my role as the agency's community educator. The members had been attentive and concerned, raising their hands with questions. How could they protect children? What were the signs of abuse in a child? Two women approached me following my presentation. They were molested as children, they said quietly. "I'm so sorry," I told them. "Thank you for your courage in telling me."

My friend introduced me and briefly described my successful lawsuit. I smiled as I greeted the audience. I glanced around, trying to make eye contact. Their eyes darted away like the minnows in a pond. Odd, I thought, as I looked out at this unresponsive group. I tapped the mike. "Can you hear me?" A few nodded politely. I began my talk with a funny story that had always generated some laughter. I might have been speaking a foreign language. I felt a chill.

I knew the audience wasn't with me as I ended my talk. They applauded politely. "Are there any questions?" No hands were raised. No one approached me when the meeting ended. No one in the room had attended the trial. Yet they had decided.

Dylan Farrow describes a similar experience. She says in a 2021 interview that it still baffles her when Woody Allen's fans come after her on Twitter saying she's lying. "This is something that I'm literally telling you happened to me. Who are you to say, 'No, it didn't'? I was there, you weren't. Go away," she tells them.[19]

Decades earlier my father had warned me, "No one will believe you." That time had come. Crimes against children had evolved from a major social problem in the 1980s to a scandalous story in the 1990s of false memories implanted by therapists. Crimes committed against children had become false memories. Even adults who had always remembered the abuse learned to be careful whom they told—if they told anyone at all. Responding to an adult's disclosure of child sexual abuse with "Oh, one of those false memories," had become the norm.

Following the trial, my attorney and I flew to Chicago. Psychologists and adults molested as children were gathering to try to figure out what to do about the false memory media coverage. At one point the speaker asked, "Doesn't anyone have any good news?" My attorney gave my shoulder a gentle push, and I walked to the front of the room. "I sued my parents. I just won a repressed memory lawsuit in Washington State," I announced. To my surprise, they applauded—a new experience for me.

"No one will believe that therapists can implant memories," many of us believed back then. We were wrong. The press and psychology textbooks had already adopted the campaign claims.

In mid-1994, Loftus quietly submitted the two-subject mall study result to the Human Subjects Review Committee.

Research corroborating recovered memories was already being published by 1994. Today, more than 20 studies, the earliest in 1987, show that recovered memories can be corroborated.[20] These data do not appear in psychology textbooks.

Psychologist Ross Cheit lists corroborated recovered memory cases at his website.[21]

Psychologist Constance Dalenberg found that adults' memories of childhood abuse are equally accurate whether recovered or always remembered.[22]

Child Maltreatment reports the average percentage of false reports of child sexual abuse for states that track such data is less than 1%.[23]

Responding to "Vanishing Facts"

> Let me tell you what false memory syndrome does to people like me, as if you care. It makes us into liars. False memory syndrome is so much more chic than child abuse . . . But there are children who tonight while you sleep are being raped, and beaten. These children may never tell because no one will believe them.

> **—Lauren Slater, quotes a survivor's letter,**
> ***Opening Skinner's Box***

The Ofshe Version—1994

After the judge's decision, I heard via the family grapevine that my mother had read a book by one of their experts, sociologist Richard Ofshe, PhD. She was telling family members she had learned things about me she didn't know. Curious, I paged through Ofshe and Ethan Watters' *Making Monsters* until I came to "Life with Father," the title I'd given the brief history of my childhood I'd written in therapy.[24]

Judge Yule had described Ofshe's testimony in the verdict, "He has resolved at the outset to find a macabre scheme of memories progressing toward satanic cult ritual and then creates them." This description applied equally well to what Ofshe had done to my life in his book. My case did not fit his false memory theory. He had cherry-picked details and edited or created others. In Ofshe's confabulated version, the corroboration had vanished. Law professor Ross Cheit, PhD, calls this phenomenon "vanishing facts," the tendency of false memory proponents to omit the corroboration in recovered memory cases.[25]

I could not sit quietly by as Ofshe lied about my case. I searched online and found nearly a dozen reviewers who had praised his book. I listed Ofshe's errors, documented my corrections, and sent a letter to each reviewer. I agreed to an interview with Katy Butler with the *Los Angeles Times* (see chapter 16). She summarized, "Inaccurate reporting like this takes a book like *Making Monsters* beyond polemic to backlash."[26]

I informed Ofshe's publisher of the errors. Ofshe agreed to one change for the second edition. He deleted "robes" from page 138.

I corrected Ofshe's version of my life in an article for the *Journal of Child Sexual Abuse* and concluded,

> I have a message for therapists who, despite the current controversy, continue to see clients they suspect were sexually abused. We are in therapy with you and that is the good news! Affirm to yourself from time to time that adults do bizarre and horrible things to children. Remember that somehow we survived. Remember that we know at some level that our survival techniques no longer work. Remember that our trauma was repressed for a very good reason and that you may trust us to recall as much as we need to recall in our own way and at our own pace.[27]

The Loftus Version—1995

Loftus misrepresented Eileen Franklin's case in 1991. She misrepresented Patti Barton's in a 1993 article for the *American Psychologist*. I was not surprised when Loftus's brief, false memory version of my case showed up in the January/February 1995 issue of *Psychology Today*. Staff reporter Jill Niemark quoted Loftus. *I testified in a case recently in a small town in the State of Washington, Loftus recalls, where the memories went from 'Daddy made me play with his penis in the shower' to 'Daddy made me stick my fist up the anus of a horse,' and they were bringing in a veterinarian to talk about just what a horse would do in that circumstance. The father is ill and will be spending close to $100,000 to defend himself."*[28]

The judge had ruled on the case a year earlier. Niemark failed to fact-check the comments of an expert who had testified for the losing side. I decided that *Psychology Today* readers, especially those who were molested as children, deserved to know the facts. I listed Loftus's errors in a letter to the magazine's editor, Hara Estroff Marano and requested a correction. Marano did not respond.

Once again, I decided to correct the record. Unlike Ofshe, Loftus was a member of the American Psychological Association (APA). I submitted an ethics complaint to the APA in December 1995. I cited the relevant APA guidelines forbidding members' misrepresentations of cases to the media. Surely, I thought, my complaint would encourage the press to fact-check the reports of cases like mine recounted by false memory adherents like Loftus.

My complaint laid out what Loftus had failed to mention—the judge declared in my favor. A sister had always remembered an incident of abuse. My father testified he didn't realize it was sexual abuse if a father made his daughter touch his penis. My father was not ill. He had testified his health was excellent. I conceded that I didn't know how much my parents' attorney and their experts had billed my parents.

Loftus may have selected the horse incident as the least credible of the 50 incidents I recalled. That memory had not surprised me. I knew of my father's interest in that area of the body. Horses or humans, it didn't matter to him. The horse, in my memory, took no notice of my father or me. My hand was small, the horse's anus was large.[29] The vet hired by my parents testified that horses are accustomed to anally inserted medications.

The December filing of my complaint coincided with the release of Loftus's long-awaited mall study.[30] Few knew that along with misrepresenting cases like mine, she had also misrepresented the mall study results. Loftus faxed her resignation to the APA on January 16, 1996. The APA allowed her to resign. Loftus maintains she was unaware of the complaints.[31]

I sent the same complaint to Loftus's department chair, psychology professor Michael Beecher. In his response, he didn't seem to know that my complaint was based on my own successful lawsuit, or that I'd shown Loftus had misrepresented my case to the media. "It is not appropriate for her department chair or any other administrator to attempt to stifle her work," Beecher replied.

Jill Niemark at *Psychology Today* called to schedule an interview. I agreed, thinking she wanted to correct the errors in her story. I was mistaken. Niemark accused me of being persuaded to file, perhaps as part of a feminist conspiracy. "No," I told her. "I filed to correct the record, and to show the importance of fact-checking the claims of false memory advocates like Loftus." Niemark told me she was "personally offended" as a feminist that I did not file a complaint against Ofshe with the APA. But Ofshe was not an APA member, I told her.

My attorney contacted the *Psychology Today* editor, suggesting that assigning the author whose article had generated an ethics complaint to write a follow-up might present a conflict of interest. Marano did not respond.

Niemark's "Dispatch from the Memory War,"[32] told readers, "If anyone should be revered by feminists and therapists, it is Loftus, a brilliant woman who has put herself on the firing line with decades of ingenious and sound research. But instead, she is violently hated by some women and psychotherapists."

If Niemark had asked me what I thought of Loftus, I would have responded, "I've never met her, but I fact-check what she says. I wish you would do the same."

The word got out about my ethics complaint. I started hearing from UW students at the conferences I attended. After Loftus's husband divorced her in 1991, she displayed behaviors that concerned the students. Students who confronted her publicly were disinvited from staff meetings. Students felt compelled to support her false memory theory to earn credit.

The Ethics Complaint Story Continues

The Hoffman Report, a review of APA psychologists' participation in the torture of prisoners at Guantanamo included a footnote on page 3274. Former APA president Gerald Koocher reported that the APA CEO, Ray Fowler, informed both him and Noreen G. Johnson in 2002 that he had advised Loftus to resign before the ethics complaint investigation could begin. He thought an ethics investigation of a high-profile psychological scientist like Loftus at that time would have severely damaged the organization (p. 3274).[33]

"He's a slimeball liar," Loftus tweeted on October 11, 2015, referring to Koocher.

The APA Honors Loftus

The American Psychological Association named its 1996 resignee, Elizabeth Loftus, as the recipient of its 2003 Distinguished Scientific Award for the Applications of Psychology. They had selected Loftus, they said, because of her "invaluable contributions in applying scientific knowledge to societal problems."[34] I was one of many who were aware of a societal problem Loftus had selected. She contributed research to support the dismissal of charges against sex offenders.

In Need of Some Fact-checking

Since false memory claims had become the norm for the media, I responded with letters to the editor that began, "This article is in need of some fact-checking." I would list three misrepresentations. I could always find at least three. I documented my corrections. One morning I telephoned a *New York Times* reporter whose recent story mentioned included Jennifer Freyd's sex abuse allegations against Peter. I told him, "Expect a call from Pamela Freyd disputing that." He replied, "She already called."

The *New York Times* published my response to Stephen Rose's positive reviews of Ofshe's *Making Monsters* and Loftus's *The Myth of Repressed Memory*. The indirect corroborative evidence in the letter is from my case.

March 26, 1995

Dear Editor:

Mr. Rose pessimistically claims that "in the absence of some independent verification procedure, there is no way of deciding between a survivor's claim that her new narrative memory is real and her father's is false."

When incest is viewed as a crime rather than as a "shocking discovery," there is often evidence that a crime has been committed. Lacking the direct evidence of a videotape of the crime or an eyewitness account, we must then rely on indirect corroborative evidence. This may include the abuse of other siblings, boundary violations of a sexual nature by the father in the family, witnesses to boundary violations from individuals outside the family, incriminating family letters, a diagnosis of post-traumatic stress disorder having no other apparent cause, initial acceptance by the mother that the abuse occurred, the defendant's inability to define correctly what sexual abuse is and is not, and inconsistencies in the defendant's testimony. This type of indirect evidence can play a significant role in helping us decide what really happened.

And if, as Mr. Rose suggests, we "let the past slip gently away," then we may also be allowing the pedophile to continue his criminal activities.

LYNN CROOK
Richland, Wash.[35]

The Gaslightings

Following Loftus's resignation from the APA in January 1996, I discovered the price of filing an ethics complaint. I was subjected to intense online harassment for months.[36] I sought support from colleagues. My husband and I discussed what we would do if any of these people showed up at our home.

When one of them called me a "bimbo," I had to smile. Little did he know that as a tall, slender brunette, I'd need an extensive makeover before anyone thought of me as a bimbo.

I've been personally attacked by *Psychology Today* columnist Jill Niemark (See Chapter 6), Frontline producer Ofra Bikel (See Chapter 7), and Elizabeth Loftus (Lost in the Mall - Misrepresentations and Understandings).

Reports of Loftus's personal attacks against me have continued sporadically over the years. I've heard that Loftus still says I'm "out to get her" because she testified for my father in 1994. No one has contacted me to confirm this. If they did, I would explain that it was the lawsuit I filed against my parents that resulted in Loftus's deposition testimony regarding the dropped six subjects that caused me to question the lost in a mall study. Loftus refers to Crook v. M. as "The Anus Case" because of the memory involving a horse. I've found that the best way for me to deal with these attacks is humor. Recently she described me as "dangerous and deceptive." That's an easier look for me than bimbo, I decided. I can picture myself dressed dramatically in black leather, maybe a pair of sunglasses . . .

Chapter 7

Frontline—The Backstory

In matters of fairness there is one specific requirement:
all producers must have a fact-checking procedure at the
completion of the program in which every line of narration
and synch and every picture is checked for the accuracy of
any factual assertion.

—*Frontline,* "Journalistic Guidelines"
(sent anonymously to *Treating Abuse Today*)

"Divided Memories"

A child's sexual relationship with an adult may have a life-long impact. Ofra Ichilof was 13 when she married Theodore Bikel, 18.[37] Their son was born shortly after the marriage. They divorced a year later. Ofra Bikel produced two docudramas for *Frontline* in 1995. Both films portray crimes committed against children as false memories.

"Divided Memories" introduced *Frontline* viewers to false memories in April 1995. The promo announced, "Bikel examines the controversy surrounding repressed memory and its use in sexual abuse cases." The *Seattle Times* called the docudrama "exhaustive research." The *Los Angeles Times* called it "an extraordinary investigation." Bikel told a reporter afterward, "I don't really care if there is such a thing as repressed memory or not—after a while I put that argument behind me."[38]

My review of "Divided Memories" for *Treating Abuse Today* (*TAT*) suggested Bikel's work would have benefitted from some fact-checking.[39] I included examples. I'd been a *Frontline* fan for years. Surely they would welcome my corrections of fact. I sent my review to *Frontline*. Series Editor Marie Campbell responded in a May 12 letter. My case was "one of hundreds of cases" preliminarily researched, she said. (They called and asked for my parents' phone number.) She closed with, "We certainly do take note of your feelings and all that you have been through." (I had successfully held my parents accountable for crimes committed against me as a child.)

Bikel responded. Her June 25 letter to *TAT* editor David Calof began, "Had we lived 200 years ago—she [Lynn Crook] would have summarily and happily sent me to be burnt at the stake." She described me as "seething with fury . . . blinded by rage . . . seething anger and contempt . . . enraged . . . a rock-thrower . . . shrill, extremely rude, highly emotional and always accusatory." *Treating Abuse Today* did not respond.

Bikel's reported inability to find corroborated cases for "Divided Memories" led attorney and political science professor Ross Cheit to establish the *Corroborated Cases of Recovered Memory Archive* online at http://blogs.brown.edu/recoveredmemory/case-archive/. The website lists over 100 cases corroborated by jury and bench decisions, witnesses, other victims, childhood reports, etc.

Bikel interviews David Calof

Seattle therapist and *Treating Abuse Today* editor David Calof had been dealing with false memory picketers for a few months when producer Ofra Bikel arrived at his office in 1995 to interview him for "Divided Memories." She asked Calof to sit with his assistant in the waiting room and converse as if they were therapist and client. Bikel explained that she wanted to show them talking with the audio turned off. As the camera was running, Calof's assistant, in an attempt at humor, turned to him and said, "I find myself dreaming about my father quite a bit and I'm trying to make sense of those dreams." Bikel aired that scene—with the audio on.[40] Calof reported the incident. *Frontline* did not respond.

Calof interviews Bikel

In a telephone interview following "Divided Memories," Calof asked Bikel why she told viewers that she had been unable to find any corroborated cases.

> **Bikel:** *But look, you have to understand something very carefully. If somebody said that they were sexually abused and even if they and the parents settled, if the father does not say that he did it, there's no way I can put it on the air. The only thing I could put on the air is exactly what happened with Jane Sanders that I had a letter from her father that he did abuse her (p. 37).*

Although Bikel had worked as a researcher for *Time, Newsweek,* and *ABC,* she explained why she didn't review any research before filming.

> **Bikel:** *I didn't see anybody's [research], Loftus, I didn't see any. I just completely, no I didn't see them. I didn't see Loftus's research, I didn't see Bessel's research. Everybody knocks everybody else's research (p. 55).*

Calof asked Bikel about a group session she aired with clients yelling and crying.

> **Calof:** *But in your piece you said, "Across the country there are counseling centers not unlike this one" and all I'm saying is, let's keep it empirical. But help me understand the sense of proportion here.*
>
> **Bikel:** *Maybe it's a mistake. Maybe I should have given a better proportion, but you know, (I had) enough to worry about (p. 28).* [41]

"The Search for Satan"

Once again, Bikel's production received positive reviews. "The Search for Satan" promo for the October program described what appeared to be a docudrama on malpractice. Both women would eventually concede under questioning that none of their memories were implanted.

Two troubled women. Both sought help from some of the top doctors in the country. The diagnosis: Satanic ritual abuse.

Mary: *It was like going deeper and deeper into an abyss.*

Announcer: *After millions of dollars in treatment, the women now say the doctors were wrong.*

Patty: *It stopped because I stopped following Dr. Braun's orders.*

Announcer: *"The Search for Satan" on FRONTLINE.*

The 1995 docudrama featured two retractors who had recently filed lawsuits against leaders in the field of trauma treatment. Mary Shanley had sued Judith Peterson, PhD, and others at Spring Shadows Glen in Houston. Pat Burgus had sued Bennett Braun and others at Rush Presbyterian in Chicago. Shanley would settle with Peterson. Then Shanley and others from the *Frontline* program would head to Houston. There they would testify in Federal Court against Peterson and others in an effort to criminalize the diagnosis and treatment of dissociative disorders.

With several insurance carriers covering the defendants in the Burgus lawsuit, a hefty settlement in the millions was expected. The settlement would encourage other patients to file malpractice lawsuits.

Fact-checking Bikel's claims about Mary Shanley was a simple matter. A few phone calls revealed that Shanley was not "listed with the State of Illinois as a child abuser" as Bikel had claimed. Shanley did not lose her teaching job because of her treatment at Spring Shadows Glen. Instead, the school district placed Shanley on full disability because of her emotional problems. She was treated at three mental health hospitals before she arrived at Spring Shadows Glen—another fact Bikel failed to mention.[42]

Burgus had introduced herself to Bikel in a letter dated August 12, 1994. She wrote, "Richard Ofshe told me to tell you that he considered you one of the greatest women—no strike that—one of the greatest people in the Western Hemisphere, and quote me." Burgus told Bikel she would have access to all her videos and hospital records.

Bikel failed to provide any details related to Burgus that I could fact-check. I would learn the rest of Burgus's story when I reviewed her deposition.

Efforts to Criminalize a Diagnosis

Three years later, Shanley testified as the government's star witness in U.S. v. Peterson. If found guilty, Peterson and the four other mental health care providers would spend the rest of their lives in prison for diagnosing patients with DID and billing through the mail.

I spent three weeks in Houston covering the trial for *Treating Abuse Today*. Perry Mason fans may recall the moment towards the end of an episode when Mason begins his cross-examination of the key suspect. His logic effectively backs the suspect into a corner. The courtroom is silent, knowing the only response left is a confession. I witnessed a similar dramatic moment in Houston as Judith Peterson's polite, gentlemanly attorney, Rusty Hardin, backed Mary Shanley into a corner after days of careful cross-examination. We sat in total silence as we awaited her response. At last, she spoke. She could not name a single memory that Peterson had implanted.

"Divided Memories" and "The Search for Satan" are available at *Turner Classic Movies*.

Chapter 8

Backstage at False Memories

My attorney deposed Elizabeth Loftus on January 24, 1994.[43] I read the deposition after the trial and stopped at:

> **Loftus:** *There were six subjects that finally finished the first study before the research assistant [James Coan] left (p. 60, Line 13-14).*

> **Levy:** *"Are you using those first six subjects as part of your study" (p. 60, Line 19-20).*

> **Loftus:** *No, not the first six (page 60, Line 21).*

Not using the first six subjects who completed a study suggested a problem. I knew from my grad school days that researchers cannot simply drop subjects like that. Curious, I telephoned Coan in August 1996. He said Loftus called him in and suggested his leadership role in the mall study might be too much for him. Jacqueline Pickrell, another undergraduate, was assigned to head the study.

Treating Abuse Today editor Ken Baker and I met with Helen McGough, manager of the Human Subjects Division, and Richard Brzustosicz, a staff person with the Division, in September 1996. We described Loftus's testimony saying she did not use the first six mall study subjects. We asked, "Was this typical?"

"No," they responded. Researchers might drop a subject if there's an illness or scheduling problem, they explained.

I solved the mystery of the six subjects years later when I read Coan's senior paper, "Creating False Memories."[44] He reported, "Of the six completed interviews," (pp. 16-17) "all subjects were able to correctly identify the false memory" (p. 16). The dropped subjects had all correctly identified the lost story as false.

In the description of his mall study experience in *Ethics & Behavior*,[45] Coan fails to mention the six subjects.

Reporting Flawed Data

There was another problem with the study.[46] The 24 subjects each received four stories, so six subjects would have to say they were lost. Instead, five subjects in the published version said they were lost (p. 723). The study had failed statistically by one. Surely the psychology community would want to know this.

I invited Martha Dean, PhD, a psychologist from Australia I'd met through *Treating Abuse Today*, to co-author a review of the mall study. Martha encouraged me to take the investigation as far as it would go. She suggested I request the annual reports Loftus had submitted to the University of Washington's Human Subjects Review Committee (HSRC).[47] We found an oddity in the final report dated June 1, 1994: 24 *subjects have been run. About 8-9% have formed false-positive memories. Another 10-15% formed partial* [48] *false memories.*" Two subjects thought they were lost? There must be some mistake. This report made no sense to us. Surely someone would have noticed if the study had failed that badly. We quoted the report in our article for *Ethics & Behavior* and left it up to someone else to figure this out.

Loftus received a copy of our article and was invited to respond. Her attorney's letter to journal editor, Gerald Koocher, PhD, stated, "Ms. Crook is a person who Professor Loftus believes has been motivated to tarnish Loftus' professional reputation ever since Loftus testified as an expert for the defense in Crook's lawsuit against her father." I wasn't interested in her reputation, I told Koocher, I was interested in her research. He published our article.

The Gaslighting

Loftus described our article as "a misrepresentation . . . a misstatement . . . a distortion . . . partisan . . . disturbing . . . unscientific . . . incompetent . . . bizarre."[49]

A personal attack like this was not what we had signed up for. We consulted with colleagues and learned we were not alone. Loftus had responded similarly to others who challenged her work.

We replied, "The *ad hominem* tone of Loftus's response follows her established strategy of response to writers who disagree with her." We provided examples. Our article, "Lost in a shopping mall—A breach of professional ethics," and our rejoinder, "Logical fallacies and ethical breaches" are online at http://users.owt.com/crook/memory.

Our "five not six" report was a minor issue compared to what was discovered years later.

The Stories They Tell

After our experience with the mall study result, Martha Dean and I decided to fact-check two of Loftus's anecdotal accounts. In *The Myth of Repressed Memory*, Loftus says she struck up a conversation with a seatmate on a flight from California to Seattle. The woman, Loftus said, was returning from Australia and New Zealand where she presented a series of lectures and workshops on surviving childhood trauma. Upon learning Loftus was a psychology professor who studied memory at the University of Washington, the woman allegedly said, "You're that woman," and swatted her over the head with the business section of *USA Today* (p. 211). Dean contacted her Australian colleagues. They knew of no one who had presented a series of lectures and workshops on childhood trauma in Australia and New Zealand.

Loftus has said that armed guards have been hired for her presentations. We tracked down one such incident. Charles Weaver, PhD, an FMS Foundation board member, was the program coordinator for the Southwestern Psychological Association (SWPA) conference in 1996. Weaver scheduled a two-hour, keynote symposium, "The False Memory Debate: Perspectives from the Cognitive Sciences."

The false memory "debaters" were all false memory advocates: John Kihlstrom, Elizabeth Loftus and Henry Roediger from the FMS Foundation, and Larry Weiskrantz from the British False Memory Society.

Several colleagues and I responded to the SWPA suggesting a new title. The panel members would not be debating each other—they agreed with each other. The symposium title was not changed, false memory critics were not added to the panel. Years later, I asked SWPA president, Roger Kirk, PhD, what happened. "The executive committee of SWPA took the complaints [about the panel selection] seriously," he said, "and hired armed security for the two sessions. Fortunately, the promised massed protests never materialized."[50]

Conference Presentations

The frequently-cited mall study was a statistical failure. Yet thousands of reports of the inflated results over the years have convinced the public that adults' child sex abuse allegations are false memories.[51]

If I didn't get the word out about this failure, adults' memories would continue to be dismissed. I joined a local Toastmasters group, thinking that might help my presentation skills, and it did. I joined a comedy improv group thinking it might help me counter any shouts from critics in the audience. No one shouted.[52]

I reported the inflated result along with my growing body of related findings at conferences in the US, Canada and Great Britain. Surely, I thought, someone would do something to stop the media's false memory coverage. Surely, reporters would want to correct their stories promoting false memories. Surely they would start fact-checking false memory claims. I reported on the costs incurred by child molesters in a presentation at the United Nations Conference on the Status of Women in 2008. At a conference in Baltimore in 2002, I showed how the testimony of three high-profile retractors who sued their therapists didn't support their implanted memory claims. Audiences applauded politely. My experience as a poster presenter at the American Psychological Association conference in 2007 was bewildering. I stood patiently at the side of my poster titled, "When ideology collides with science." I made eye contact with approaching members. They skirted around me. No one stopped to discuss the findings. One woman approached me, said "Controversial," then strode on.

As I became known as a survivor who prevailed in a lawsuit and then fact-checked false memory claims, I was invited to appear in documentaries. Representatives from the Korean Broadcasting System arrived at my home in 2011 to film *Memory*. I told the interviewer, "My memory kept me safe as a child. As an adult, my memory became my teacher." Filmmaker Mary Knight arrived in 2016 to film *Am I Crazy? My Journey to Determine If My Memories Are True*. Her film has been viewed over 100,000 times.

In 2019, researcher Linda McEwen and I analyzed the mall study in depth. We arrived at a conclusion that seemed anticlimactic. The 24 subjects had *all* identified the "lost" story as false. No false memories were implanted. We titled our article for the *Journal of Child Custody*, "Deconstructing the lost in the mall study."[53] Psychologists Ruth Blizard and Morgan Shaw's "Lost-in-the-mall: False memory or false defense?"[54] that same year reported a similar result. Loftus told an interviewer that the articles were a "smear" and refused to discuss them.

The Last Conference—2002

I was invited to Chicago to review documents related to an earlier malpractice lawsuit. I scheduled my visit so I could attend what turned out to be the final FMS Foundation conference. I registered under my maiden name, hoping to avoid notice as someone who had filed an ethics complaint against Loftus. About 150 attendees were present at the hotel in Glenview. I didn't see anyone who might be a journalist.

I found a seat at the back of the room where I overheard two women saying, "She's amazing, so wonderful!" This was the first of many comments I would hear during the two-day conference suggesting the members idolized Loftus.

During a morning break, I recognized Pat Burgus who had attended the criminal trial in Houston. She stood at Loftus's side on the other side of the room, pointing in my direction. Busted!

Loftus was among friends so I was curious to hear what she had to say about Nicole Taus, a young Navy pilot who had just sued her and others associated with Loftus's "Jane Doe" article in the *Skep-*

tical Inquirer.[55] Towards the end of the presentation, Loftus asked her audience in a disapproving tone, "Can you believe this? Jane is in the Navy representing our country. *Dateline* is interested in the story." The audience applauded. "The *Dateline* producer did one of the early shows sympathetic to Eileen Franklin," (See Chapter 10) Loftus said, adding, "This is her chance to redeem herself."

I took notes as another speaker directed parents to turn self-help books spine in at Barnes & Noble. "Move *Sybil*, Renee Fredrickson's *Repressed Memories* and *The Courage to Heal* to the fiction section," she instructed. One speaker happily reported they had gotten a counselor in Colorado fired, and the "troublemakers" out. They were getting a group together to picket *Courage to Heal* co-author Ellen Bass's presentation in a nearby city.

Foundation board member Paul McHugh assured the audience that the priest abuse cases getting all the media attention that year were different from the accusations against Foundation members. The priests' accusers were older at the time of the abuse, he said, and they were male.

A casually dressed Peter Freyd strode towards me during a break, his camera aimed in my direction. I ducked my head, turned, and found my way to a smaller room. A pleasant-looking couple approached a few minutes later and asked if they could join me. I nodded and gestured to two empty chairs at the table. They asked me why I was there. "Because a family member recovered memories," I said, the response I'd prepared in case anyone asked that question. The couple told me their story of a family torn apart by false accusations.

During another break, I saw author Mark Pendergrast seated in the hotel lobby surrounded by parents. I watched as he invited them to contribute their stories for a book.

I sat in on a discussion titled, "Risks and Benefits of Going Public" moderated by Larry Koszewski. Based on the reports I heard from the parents, going public seemed more beneficial than risky for these accused parents. They were telling a story the public wanted to hear—parents don't molest their children.

The Human Subjects Review Committee Report

Back at home following the Foundation's conference in 2002, I was sorting through some old files when I came across Loftus's final report to the Human Subjects Review Committee. I read it again. *24 subjects have been run. About 8-9% have formed false-positive memories. Another 10-15% have formed partial false memories. The memories appear to be less clear and vivid than true memories.*

Her report meant exactly what it said, I realized. The result was 8-9%, or two subjects, a "by chance" result. Loftus informed the Committee that her mall study had failed. It wasn't memory that was unreliable. It was the mall study result.

Telling the Story

My experience at the agency had shown me that we support the accused child molesters we know. We effectively cover up their crimes by silencing their victims with advice, shunning and personal attacks. During the 1990s and beyond we effectively silenced adults molested as children by insisting their memories are false.

In 2019 I switched my focus from reporting data to telling the story of how the false memory defense was created by a PhD, and then promoted by accused parents. I presented the story at the International Society for the Study of Trauma and Dissociation Conference in New York. I explained how the accused parents needed a defense after states passed laws allowing adults molested as children to sue for damages. They selected "implanted by therapists" after the *Washington Post* headlined the story.

I told the group how psychologist Elizabeth Loftus introduced the false memory story to individual journalists. I told them about the non-profit the parents founded, and then invested millions in a campaign to promote themselves as falsely accused. I described how those who challenged the parents' false claims were gaslighted, threatened, harassed and litigated. I named Loftus's recent celebrity clients and told attendees I'd consulted with the prosecutors preparing to cross-examine Loftus. I closed by saying it's time for us to say farewell to a defense that was introduced and promoted by accused child molesters. The audience stood to applaud. They asked questions. I returned home to Seattle with the realization that I had a book to write.

PART 2

The Silencing

Prologue

"The role of reporters is to go where the silence is and say something," says investigative journalist Amy Goodman.[56] Reporters in the 1980s went to where the silence was and said our children are being molested by people we know.

Parents accused of molesting their children took center stage in the 1990s. They established a charity, donated millions, and told us tragic tales of families torn apart by false accusations.

What follows is about a crime that impacts the lives of millions, a crime that our culture has tolerated for a very long time, a crime that horrifies and disgusts us. It's a crime that's committed by people we may know, by people we may care about, by people we just can't believe would ever do anything like that to a child.

It's about the emotional and physical costs that adults molested as children must bear, and the emotional and financial burdens we all must bear because of the harm child molesters cause to all of us.

It's about an inconvenient crime, one that if we report it will disrupt our family or our church or our school—and our lives.

It's about a media network that influences our beliefs about child molesters and their victims.

It's about those who insist those crimes never happened, they're false memories.

Chapter 9

Generational Reckonings with Families

Some social problems are so widespread, so intertwined with our families and institutions, that they cannot be easily resolved. Instead, they are addressed until a counter-response begins. Reporting laws in the 1970s caused child sex abuse reports to skyrocket by the early 1980s. The decade became a time of cultural reckoning of the damage caused by child molesters within families. The children had promised they would never tell. They had not spoken of the abuse in decades. Surely, they had forgotten. Then as adults in the 1980s, they made independent choices to speak out, free of the emotional bond that had kept them silent as children. The media listened.

ABC Theater aired "Something About Amelia" in January 1984. An unspeakable topic became speakable—incest in a middle-class family. "Ted Danson's intense yet slightly distant Steven, Glenn Close's reluctantly comprehending Gail, and Miss Zal's heartbroken Amelia add up to a television project of unusual power," a *New York Times* reviewer said.[57] Thousands called help lines following the program. "Something About Amelia" received three Grammys.

The Associated Press released Robert T. Pienciak's five-part series on child sexual abuse, "America's Dirty Little Secret." He described our reaction to child molesters, "We tolerate their behavior. We dispense weak punishment."[58]

Marvel Comics' "Secrets" featured Spider-Man and the Power

Pack helping children who were forced or tricked by an older person into sexual contact.[59]

The *Los Angeles Times* surveyed 2,627 adults across the country in 1985 and reported, "22% in survey were child abuse victims."[60] More than two-thirds knew the offender. Three percent of the cases were reported to authorities. The report suggested that child molesters had accessed millions of victims. A survey by John Briere and Marsha Runtz found that 21 percent of men are sexually attracted to young children.[61]

A woman in Washington State took the next step.

Patti Barton: Holding Them Accountable

Her father called it "tickling." The courts called it a crime. It isn't right, Patti Barton, 34, told herself one morning as she sat at her kitchen table paying the household bills. Her young family shouldn't have to suffer financially so she could see a therapist to recover from the consequences of her father's crime. She asked her father, a former church pastor, to pay for her therapy. He refused.

Patti's husband, Kelvin, picked up the phone and called their state legislator. Could a law be introduced to allow adults more time to hold child molesters accountable?

The lobbying efforts of the Bartons and others resulted in the Revised Code of Washington (RCW) 4.16.340 in 1988.[62] The new law provided a three-year window for adults to hold the offender accountable and sue for damages. The charges could be based on either *delayed discovery* of the abuse or *delayed recognition of the harm* caused by the abuse. The door to justice now stood open for adults in Washington State.

Patti's parents didn't respond to her settlement offer. Instead, they packed up and moved to Alaska. The Bartons followed and successfully lobbied the Alaska state legislature. Barton's father hired attorney Dick Madsen to represent him and University of Washington psychology professor Elizabeth Loftus to provide expert testimony. Barton's father agreed to a pretrial settlement.[63]

The Bartons contacted every state legislature and lobbied many of them to allow victims to sue for damages. By 1992 when the accused parents went public with their false memory claims, Alaska, California, Colorado, Illinois, Iowa, Maine, Maryland, Minnesota, Missouri, Montana, Nevada, Oregon, South Dakota, Washington, and Vermont allowed adults molested as children to sue for damages.[64]

The False Memory Version

The American Psychological Association's *American Psychologist* was the first to publish a false memory version of a case without verifying the account. "The Reality of Repressed Memory" is posted at Loftus's dormant University of Washington website.[65]

"Elizabeth Loftus had the records, so she was familiar with my case," Barton explains. "Her article in the *American Psychologist* left out the fact that I always remembered what my father told me he was doing when he molested me—he was tickling me." She added, "Loftus claimed my therapist used visualization to try to get me to remember my past. That's false. My therapist told me to think of a familiar place that felt safe to me. That helped me to feel less fearful when I spoke about my childhood. I remembered the abuse on my own, without any help from my therapist."

The Consequences of Going Public

The Bartons experienced years of personal attacks, stalking, anonymous letters, and middle-of-the-night obscene phone calls from family members and perhaps others. Her father had become the 'innocent' victim of her accusations. "It was like being bullied for reporting a crime, Patti says today, "If I could do it all over again, I would still lobby to change the law. Victims have a right to hold their offenders accountable." She sighs. "I just wish we would have moved our children away from those people a lot sooner."

The Bartons support Dawson Place, an organization in Everett that enables molested children to find support and healing from trauma. They also support the Promise 23 Ministries Ranch in Everson. The organization works with sex trafficking victims through equine therapy. Kelvin continues to communicate with state legislators across the country about civil remedies for victims of child sex abuse. The Bartons say they particularly enjoy the reports of cases from across the country that would have been barred prior to their landmark work.

Eileen Franklin: Exhuming the Memory

Can a child survive an overwhelming, traumatic event by archiving the memory, by repressing it until the memory is triggered by a similar event in adulthood? The Franklin case introduced amnesia for childhood trauma to the legal arena.

The body of eight-year-old Susan Nason was discovered in 1969 at Crystal Springs Reservoir in California.[66] Twenty years later, Eileen Franklin Lipsker, a red-haired mother of two, glanced down at her red-haired, blue-eyed young daughter and suddenly recalled witnessing her father rape and murder her best friend, red-haired, blue-eyed Susan Nason. Eileen explained, "The moment I caught my daughter's eyes, those big blue eyes, all of a sudden it was Susan's blue eyes. Inside I shouted, 'No!' But it was not to be stopped, it was too late."[67] Her father threatened to kill her if she ever told anyone about what he had done to Susan.[68]

Eileen reported what she remembered to authorities. Detectives reviewed the sheriff's and coroner's files and compared the details to Eileen's report. Consistent with Eileen's recollection, the coroner's files noted that two rings, one missing a stone on her crushed hand, were found on the body. The media reports stated that one ring was found. The reports did not mention the other ring or Susan's crushed hand—information that Eileen had provided. Susan's remains lay underneath a box spring mattress as Eileen had described. Susan had been hit twice, Eileen said, another detail the media did not mention. The coroner's report validated Eileen's report. George Franklin, a retired firefighter, was arrested and charged with murder. Exhibit C, in the possession of the defendant at the time of his arrest, included nineteen child-pornography items. Similar items were found in his storage locker in Sacramento.

Eileen testified. Her therapist testified he had not hypnotized Eileen, Lenore Terr, MD, testified for the prosecution. Elizabeth Loftus, PhD, and David Spiegel, MD, testified for the defense. The jury found George Franklin guilty of first-degree murder on November 30, 1990. The decision validated the memories of an eight-year-old child who had witnessed a shocking, traumatic event.

The defense appealed the decision. The California Supreme Court upheld the jury's decision on April 15, 1993, ruling that Franklin could not substantiate his claim that Eileen's recovered memories were the result of hypnosis. Following a second appeal, the Ninth Circuit Court of Appeals ruled that Franklin was deprived of his Fifth Amendment right to remain silent and his Sixth Amendment right to counsel. George's conviction was vacated on April 4, 1995. The vacated conviction did not suggest George was innocent, only that he was deprived of certain rights.

Following his release in July 1996, George Franklin sued his daughter and the others involved in the prosecution of his case. His lawsuits were dismissed.

A detailed discussion of the case is online at the website of the US Court of Appeals, Ninth Circuit.[69]

People magazine's "Exhuming the Horror" recounted the story of Eileen and her father.[70] "Fatal Memories," starring Shelly Long as Eileen and Duncan Fraser as George, aired in 1992. Eileen's memoir, *Sins of the Father*, was reprinted in four languages. She was an invited speaker at the American College for Psychiatrists in 1992 and the Washington State Associations of Police Chiefs and Sheriffs in 1993. She appeared on more than two dozen talk shows in the US, England, and Ireland.

The False Memory Versions

Following the trial, defense expert Elizabeth Loftus incorrectly told a *Toronto Star* reporter in 1991, "All of the daughter's memories were things that had been made public."[71] Loftus followed up with a dramatic revenge motive for Eileen in *The Myth of Repressed Memory*. Eileen allegedly punished her father for his "cruel, abusive treatment of her family" (p. 71). The chapter was excerpted in *Cosmopolitan* magazine.[72]

Perhaps Eileen was suspicious when *Dateline* contacted her in 1995. She had already turned down two earlier invitations to appear on the program. Host Maria Shriver asked, "If you don't tell your story, then who will?" Eileen agreed to an interview. *Dateline's*

"Remember When" aired on March 21, 1995. Sociologist Richard Ofshe introduced the program: "It is reckless. It is dangerous. It is wrong. Recovered memory therapy is the psychiatric psychological quackery of the 20th century."

George Franklin did not testify during the trial. However, he agreed to an in-prison interview with Shriver, answering only preapproved questions. They walked together across prison grounds for the interview.

> **Shriver:** *(Voiceover) This is the first time George Franklin has ever spoken about his case. He would only answer limited questions.*

> **Mr. Franklin:** *It's an incredible, bizarre hoax. And I deal with it as well as I know how.*

> **Shriver:** *What is an incredible, bizarre hoax?*

> **Mr. Franklin:** *This so-called repressed memory notion.*

Eileen's was not the story Shriver wanted to tell. Eileen notified *Dateline* of the errors in Shriver's portrayal of the case. *Dateline* did not respond.

Dateline effectively silenced Eileen. She refused further interview requests.

Fact-Checking for the Press

Would reporters correct their errors? I decided to see if journalists would revise their coverage of the Franklin case if they were provided with substantiated corrections. I contacted three writers and quoted their errors. I included corrections for their errors with a link to the appeals court decision so they could fact-check the correction I suggested.

Emma Bryce with *Wired UK* claimed the judge overturned the conviction because Eileen's sister, Janice, testified that Eileen had recovered the memories during hypnotherapy sessions.[73] I showed that the court had dismissed the hypnosis claim based on the lack of evidence.[74] Bryce did not correct the error.

Guardian staff writer Holly Watt wrote, "In 1996, amid doubts over his daughter's testimony, Franklin was exonerated."[75] I documented that Franklin was not exonerated. The verdict was vacated (rendered moot) due to violations of Franklin's Fifth and Sixth Amendment rights. Watt did not correct the error.

Chris Woolston with *Knowable Magazine* claimed Eileen remembered the murder incident while under hypnosis. The editor agreed to one change and stated that it's "unclear whether she was under hypnosis."[76]

Thirty years later, the media is still intent on reporting the false memory version of a story told by a beautiful, articulate, thirty-year-old redhead who accused her father of murder based upon a recovered memory. *Showtime* resurrected the Franklin case in October 2021 as "Buried," a four-part series. The producers offered viewers a SODDI (Some Other Dude Did It) version and a speculative approach, "She accused him because she . . ." The producers failed to discuss the decision of the US Court of Appeals, Ninth Circuit. They failed to cite the research on amnesia related to childhood trauma.

George Franklin died in 2016.

Textbooks and the Franklin Case

> "A lot of times trauma is just stored in our bodies, and we've disassociated. Fight, flight, freeze. Later on, we can melt and come through, when it might feel like a safer choice to make. It's quite traumatic to not only relive it but then to be in the public eye and have it questioned."

—Alanis Morissette, "Reckoning," 2020

Psychology students are told Eileen's memories are false. The Gleitman textbook (2010) displays a photo of Eileen and George with the caption, "New evidence (unspecified) emerged showing that he could not have committed the crime." The Coon textbook (2015) claims George Franklin was cleared based on DNA testing. *Psychological Science* (2015) claims, "Evidence subsequently emerged proving his innocence." Similar claims can be found at the *National Registry of Exonerations*[77] and the *Jewish Family Weekly* websites.

Celebrities Remember: 1991

> "The media was the catalyst that helped to free thousands of
> men and women from their secrets and their shame."

> —**Marilyn Van Derbur Atler,** *Miss America by Day,* **2003**

Following the Franklin verdict, celebrities went public with disclosures of childhood sex abuse. They named the offenders—their fathers. They told their own stories. No false memory experts were called upon to speculate. Their mothers knew about the abuse. They described the long-term consequences of the abuse—addictions, PTSD, depression, and neurological problems. The message was clear to the millions who were molested as children: "Incest harms children. It's okay to tell."

Accused parents dismissed the celebrity cases. Their newsletter asked, "Does anyone doubt that there is also 'copy-catting' when celebrities come forth to describe their recovered memories of childhood abuse?"[78]

Sandra Dee: America's Sweetheart

A *People* magazine cover on March 18, 1991, announced, "Look at me, I'm Sandra Dee. She was America's teen sweetheart of the '50s—then she disappeared. For the first time, she now reveals the shocking details of her two lost decades."

> Dee was 8 when her mother married a wealthy, older man. "While my mother was dating him, he began fondling me. After they got married, it got worse . . . He had me sleep in the middle," Dee said. At 18, Dee married Bobby Darin. "I thought I had blocked out the abuse, but on my wedding night it all came back."[79]

Hospitalized for alcoholism and weight loss in 1989, Dee died in 2005 due to complications from kidney disease.

Marilyn Van Derbur Atler: Miss America by Day

A June 18 *People* magazine cover announced, "A Story of Incest: Miss

America's Triumph Over Shame. It began at age 5. Now Marilyn Van Derbur tells of her shocking 13-year ordeal of sexual abuse by her millionaire father."

When she was twenty-four, Marilyn Van Derbur Atler recalled the abuse during a conversation with a former youth pastor. Marilyn told her older sister what she'd remembered. Her sister replied, "Oh no, I thought I was the only one!" When Atler's daughter was five—her age when her father started molesting her—Atler began experiencing bouts of paralysis. She sought therapy.

"There will always be people who will not believe survivors of childhood abuse," Atler writes in *Miss America by Day*. She calls them "bullies." Many survivors are bullied by family members and others who say, "I don't believe you," or "Stop lying," or "Don't ever say those words again." She declares, "Bullies help define one of the most important purposes of my life: to stand strong and tall for those who simply cannot, yet, oppose the bullies" (p. 336).

Atler's in-laws were aware of her spells of paralysis and anxiety. After the death of her father, her mother-in-law advised Marilyn that her paralysis spells were difficult for her husband and daughter. She added, "Bootsie (Atler's mother) told me what causes these spells. Greed over the estate. I'm hoping you can find a way to let this go."

When she heard that explanation, Atler said she began to understand how "sweetly vicious" her mother was when it came to sacrificing her daughter to save herself. "She needed to believe she was the perfect wife and mother, and incest didn't fit in that picture" (p. 258).

Atler continues to educate the public on the long-term consequences for the millions of adults who were molested as children.[80]

The Miss America organization adopted the platform concept for contestants in 1989. Mallory Hytes, the 2013 Miss America, featured a sexual abuse awareness and prevention platform.

Challenging an Expert

"I am a human trafficking survivor. My parents were my pimps," filmmaker Mary Knight tells audiences today. Like many children, Knight managed to repress her memories of the abuse. At thirty-seven, she remembered. At fifty-seven, she initiated a discussion. With a camera running, she interviewed both skeptics and believers of the ability of children to archive traumatic incidents until they reach adulthood. She concludes the incidents happened.[81] Her parents trafficked her. She tells us, "It saves kids' lives to listen to survivors."

Knight became the first interviewer to challenge the claims of memory researcher Elizabeth Loftus. Knight prepared for the interview by reviewing Marilyn Van Derbur Atler's own account of her life in *People* magazine.[82] Knight's gentle questioning demonstrated that Loftus appeared unwilling to concede any evidence that supported Atler's claims.

> **Knight:** *In 1958, she became Miss America, and in 1964, she remembered the abuse.*
>
> **Loftus:** *She went through a tremendous amount of all kinds of different therapy before, highly suggestive therapy before she told the story of abuse.*
>
> **Knight:** *So, that's not what was reported in People magazine. Is there some other way you have to, way you have to—*
>
> **Loftus:** *I've watched lectures that she's given.*
>
> **Knight:** *And in lectures, she's said what?*
>
> **Loftus:** *She's talked about the massive amount of therapy.*
>
> **Knight:** *But that was not, that was after remembering.*
>
> **Loftus:** *I'm not sure of that. No.*
>
> **Knight:** *Uh-huh. And then her sister of course always remembered.*
>
> **Loftus:** *Well, we don't know exactly what the sister remembers. I've never read what the sister remembers. The sister supposedly remembers, felt there was some kind of abuse.*[83]

Others Speak Out

After Mackenzie Phillips, an American actor and singer, reported sexual abuse by her father on *Oprah* in 2009, the *Rape, Abuse & Incest National Network* (RAINN) hotline reported a 26 percent increase in calls. Calls to the National Sexual Assault *Online* Hotline increased by 83 percent. Phillips received hundreds of letters telling her, "Now I know I'm not alone."[84]

AnnaLynne McCord from *90210* actress tells survivors, "Don't let the polite lies of society silence you. Honestly, I would endure everything all over again—it has led me to my own revolution."[85] Celebrity disclosures continue—Lady Gaga, Ashley Judd, Carlos Santana, Oprah Winfrey, Tyler Perry, Queen Latifah, Teri Hatcher, Axl Rose, Sally Field . . .

Chapter 10

In Search of a Defense

A dozen state legislatures allowed adults molested as children to sue for damages by 1991. Millions of adults were eligible to file lawsuits.[86] Accused parents struggled to find a response for these charges.

1. Gaslight the Accuser

> "Allowing alleged incest perpetrators to define repressed memory is like allowing Harvey Weinstein to define sexual trauma. Abusers have been calling their victims crazy since the dawn of time. Loftus lent authority to that diagnosis."
>
> **—Anna Holzman, *Harvey Weinstein's "False Memory" Defense and Its Shocking Origin Story*, 2020**

The temperature was below freezing in December 1990 when Jennifer Freyd, thirty-three, a research psychologist and professor at the University of Oregon, headed for her first appointment with a licensed psychologist. She had been feeling increasingly anxious at the thought of her parents' upcoming holiday visit, but she didn't know why. Her father, Peter, fifty-four, was a math professor at the University of Pennsylvania. Her mother, Pamela, fifty-two, worked part-time for the Philadelphia School District as a computers-in-education expert.

Midway into the second session, the psychologist asked Jennifer if she had ever been sexually abused. "No," she said. Then she paused for a moment and began listing examples of her father's sexually inappropriate behavior, his sexual talk, wearing his robe in a manner that exposed his genitals, suggesting she read *Lolita*[87] at age nine or ten, using her to demonstrate how adults kiss during a high-school play rehearsal . . .[88]

Within a few hours, Jennifer, who had not read *The Courage to Heal* or undergone hypnosis, was at home, overwhelmed by memories of sexual abuse by her father.

After Pamela and Peter's arrival, Peter saw his two-year-old grandson holding a turkey baster. He explained to him how lesbians use turkey basters to inseminate themselves.[89] Pamela dismissed Peter's comment as good-humored, open, family discussion.[90, 91] At Jennifer's request, her husband asked her parents to return home to Philadelphia. He told them Jennifer was remembering that her father had molested her. Peter responded, "I have no memory for that."

Pamela was angry. Back at home after the aborted visit, she got to work. "Turning my anger to action has surely helped," she said. "How Could This Happen? Coping with a False Accusation of Incest and Rape" by "Jane Doe" appeared six months later in *Issues of Child Abuse Accusations*, a journal co-edited by Ralph Underwager, PhD, and Hollida Wakefield, MA.[92]

Gaslighting is a form of bullying designed to cause individuals to question their sanity. Accused child molesters use gaslighting to encourage others to question the sanity of their accuser. Writing as "Jane Doe," Pamela described "Susan" as "cruel," "dramatic," "Gestapo-like," having "some kind of a nervous breakdown" (p. 155), and "insulting," "degrading," and "temporarily deranged" (p. 158).

Pamela sent copies of her article to Jennifer's colleagues and the administrators at the University of Oregon. The article included enough information for recipients to identify "Susan" as Jennifer Freyd. "Jane" explained why her husband could not be guilty. "I've known him since he was nine years old." Stepsiblings Pamela and Peter met as children during a lengthy affair between Pamela's mother and Peter's father that ended in marriage. Shortly before Pamela and Peter met, Peter, then nine, was sent by his parents to Patzcuaro,

Mexico, to spend the summer with Gino Conti, forty-five, an artist friend of his parents. Peter described his summer experience with Conti as "precocious sexuality."[93] At sixteen, Peter began teaching at the Conti Art School in Providence, Rhode Island.[94] Conti's murals depicting underdressed Greek youth were uncovered during a 2010 renovation at Rhode Island State College.[95, 96]

Pamela's attempt to portray her husband as falsely accused to Jennifer's colleagues was unsuccessful. The media did not cover her story. Jennifer terminated contact with her parents. The Freyds' ethics complaint filed against Jennifer's therapist was dismissed.[97]

Jennifer spoke publicly at a conference in Ann Arbor, Michigan, in August 1993. Her talk is excerpted in *Blind to Betrayal* (2013), co-authored by Freyd and Pamela Birrell. She said she did not read *The Courage to Heal* until after she recalled the memories. Birrell's open letter to the board members of the False Memory Syndrome Foundation appears in *Blind to Betrayal*. Birrell says that two members responded. "Their responses were terse and uncompromising . . . and [they] were not willing to engage in dialogue."

Jennifer is credited with creating DARVO (deny, attack, reverse victim and offender). The term describes the phenomenon of accused perpetrators who portray themselves as a victim of false accusations.

Harvard University Press published Jennifer's *Betrayal Trauma: The Logic of Forgetting Childhood Abuse*. The book was positively reviewed by *The New York Times* and by Sylvia Fraser with the *Globe and Mail*.[98]

Pamela threatened a lawsuit against the *Globe* unless her side was presented. The newspaper conceded, and columnist Margaret Wente responded with "Recovered Memory: What's Real, What's Not."

Jennifer co-authored *Blind to Betrayal: Why We Fool Ourselves; We Aren't Being Fooled* in 2013 with Pamela Birrell.[99] Freyd received a Guggenheim fellowship and served twice as a fellow at Stanford University's Center for the Advancement of Behavioral Sciences. She is an adjunct professor at Stanford Medical School and a fellow at the Clayman Institute for Gender Research at Stanford University. She is a member of the National Academies of Science's advisory committee for the Action Collaborative on Preventing Sexual Harassment in Higher Education. She serves as editor for the *Journal of Trauma &*

Dissociation. As a fellow at Stanford University, she conducted a symposium at the university's Center for Advanced Study in the Behavioral Sciences titled "Betrayal and Courage in the Age of #MeToo." Freyd is the founder of The Center for Institutional Courage, which encourages institutions to become more accountable, equitable, and effective places for everyone.

Pamela and Peter Freyd are retired and live in Philadelphia.

2. Enlist the Media

> "The notion that therapists can implant scenarios of horror in the minds of their patients resonates with popular fears of manipulation by therapists and popular stereotypes of women as irrational, suggestible, or vengeful. It appeals to the common wish to deny or minimize the reality of sexual violence."

—Judith L. Herman and Mary R. Harvey, "The False Memory Debate: Social Science or Social Backlash," 1993

"They're suspicious," Elizabeth Loftus, PhD, said, describing memories of childhood trauma to a reporter from the *Toronto Star* in early 1991.[100] "They're driven by hatred and revenge," she told a *Seattle P-I* reporter in early May.[101] "Memories of sex abuse are unreliable," a *Free Lance-Star* reporter quoted her in late May.[102] Loftus had proposed, "A young woman who is sexually attracted to her father may try to repress her disturbing incestuous desires" in a 1981 textbook.[103] She tried a similar approach in a *Washington Post* interview in August, "An overly zealous psychologist could unwittingly use his or her influence over a vulnerable patient to plant the seeds of a 'memory' that is actually a fantasy."

The *Post* didn't question the story. They dropped "fantasy" and headlined the story as, "Delayed Lawsuits of Sexual Abuse on the Rise: Alleged Victims Basing Actions on Memories Critics Say May Be Implanted in Therapy."[104]

The *LA Times* followed with, "Victims say their memories of the horrors were repressed for decades. Critics speak of fantasy and distortion."[105] The reporter made it seem easy. She wrote, "False memories [of childhood sexual assault] can be planted through tone of voice or the phrasing of a question," citing George Ganaway, PhD, and others.

Two major newspapers had supported Loftus's new version of child sex abuse allegations. Loftus would use the "implanted in therapy" approach to defend the middle-class parents she would call, "victims of false accusations."

Parents accused by their younger children also claimed they were falsely accused. They joined forces in the 1990s and claimed the other parent had "alienated" the child. They called it Parental Alienation.

3. Expanding the False Memory Story

Pamela Freyd and her colleagues added details to the implanted memory story. A decade earlier, Pamela had contacted Philadelphia psychiatrist Howard Lief, MD, who had referred her husband for alcoholism treatment. When she contacted Lief about the sex abuse allegations in late 1991, he invited the Freyds to his office for an interview with Darrell Sifford, a nationally syndicated columnist with *The Philadelphia Inquirer*.

Sifford's "Accusations of Sex Abuse, Years Later," on November 24, 1991, quoted an anonymous Pam Freyd, whose version now included *The Courage to Heal*. "[Pamela] said that the therapist had given her daughter a copy of *The Courage to Heal* on the daughter's third visit and that the daughter shortly thereafter had begun to remember childhood sexual abuse."

He quoted Lief, whose version included hypnosis. "The daughter had remembered the events during therapy when she was under hypnosis," he told Sifford.

Hollida Wakefield contributed "tidy explanation." She said, "Women who remember these events [of childhood sexual abuse] years later do have problems, and the 'abuse' offers a tidy explanation for their problems."

Sifford's January column, "When Tales of Sex Abuse Aren't True," included contact information: "The Institute for Psychological Therapies in Northfield, Minn. has a toll-free telephone line for parents who have been falsely accused of sexual abuse by their children. The number is 800-568-8882."

3. The Evidence

> A teenager is convinced by his older brother that he was
> lost as a child when they were at the mall in Spokane with
> their family. Perhaps we can identify with that experience.
> Perhaps we can remember our own confusion and fear when
> we lost sight of our parents. Experts tell us this mall story is
> evidence that therapists can implant memories of childhood
> sexual assault in their clients.
>
> **—A Parable**

Loftus needed evidence to support her false memory theory. She offered an extra credit assignment to her fall quarter cognitive psychology students in 1991. James Coan, then a junior, described the assignment.

> She noted that it would be extremely interesting, and import-
> ant to the repression debate if it were possible to get some-
> body to remember an entire event that had never happened.
> She offered extra credit points (5, I believe) toward our final
> grade in the class for designing and piloting a method of
> making somebody believe they had been lost in a shopping
> mall.[106]

Loftus did not direct her students to come up with an approach that a therapist might use. Instead, two of her students created detailed, credible, false stories for their younger relatives. Coan implied he had witnessed the mall incident. He told his mother and younger brother,

> It was 1981 or 1982. I remember that Chris was five.
> We had gone shopping at the University City shopping
> mall in Spokane.[107] I was twelve. Somehow, we had lost
> Chris. After some panic, we found Chris being led down
> the mall by a tall, oldish man (I think he was wearing
> a flannel shirt). Chris was crying and holding the man's
> hand. The man explained that he found Chris walking
> around, crying his eyes out just a few minutes before,
> and was trying to help him find his parents.[108, 109]

Coan asked his family members to write about the three true stories and the false story for five days, then summarize what they remembered. His mother did not remember Chris getting lost.[110] His younger brother said he got lost and added details to the false story. Loftus describes further false memory implantations using younger relatives in *The Myth of Repressed Memory* (pp. 95, 99). She selected Coan's story to present to the media. Coan, a junior, returned for winter quarter at the University of Washington in 1992 and learned he had been appointed to head the mall study.

The claim that adults' child sex abuse allegations were implanted by therapists was based on the Big Lie technique. Tell a story that distorts the truth, and everyone will believe it must be true. No one would promote a lie like that. Repeat the story. The press didn't question Loftus's story. If Coan convinced his younger brother that he witnessed him getting lost, then surely therapists can convince clients they were sexually assaulted as a child by a family member.

Chapter 11

A Charity for Accused Parents

"The perpetrator was fairly guaranteed that he would
never be caught or successfully prosecuted. Now
women—and men—have begun to use the courts to
hold them accountable for the first time, and we see the
perpetrators fighting back.

**—Judith Herman, MD, American Psychiatric
Association meeting, 1994**

Accused parents facing possible lawsuits established a nonprofit in
March 1992. They were falsely accused of sexual assault by their
adult children, they said. They were victims of false accusations.
They called their charity the False Memory Syndrome Foundation.

Early Foundation newsletters show how the parents presented
false memories to the media as science, rather than as a PR campaign
with a budget in the millions. Their claims were scientific, they said.
"Memory is not reliable, it's a creative process, a reconstruction."[111]
The parents explained, "There is an important distinction between
bringing child sexual abuse to light in the public forum—as it should
be, and encouraging delusional thinking by making heroines of [millions of] people who see things that are not there."

The parents failed to address victim prevalence. Approximately one
in 5 women, and one in 10 men, over 40 million adults, are molested
as children.[112] Apparently, all those accusations were false memories.

This was not a "talk-show debate" with both sides presenting their ideas, the parents insisted. There was just one side—theirs. The accusations *are* false memories, they insisted. In the view of the parents, adults accusing their parents of incest had created a "very dangerous situation."[113] Middle-class parents outing themselves like this was convincing. Surely these parents would not go public like this unless the accusations were false.

Academics who disagree with false memory claims don't know what the memory debate is about, the Foundation insisted. False memory advocates were backed by established science. The group dismissed the other side as a sociopolitical movement claiming children can repress incidents of childhood trauma (May 1996).

They insisted on "balanced" media coverage. With false reports averaging five percent or less,[114] false memory advocates insisted the media concede that the accusations could be false. Some editors still insist on "balance." Josh Kendall's 2021 article for the *Scientific American* reports that *MRI scans support the amnesia-related arguments of clients and trauma therapists.*[115] *The "balanced" article quoted psychology* professor Henry Otgaar who said the brain-imaging studies support just the *claims* of patients who said they had experienced trauma.

Who Will Lead Them?

Peter Freyd announced the names of the Foundation's co-founders in a March 3, 1995, post to witchhnt@mit.edu. "There is no secret that the three couples (Brewster, Orne, and Freyd) who did set up the Foundation had previously established a toll-free number." Pamela Freyd introduced herself to the members as their executive director in a February 1992 newsletter. She had a PhD in education, she told them.

An executive board was named:

Robert Koscielny, Ohio
Lee Arning, New York
Nancy Brewster, Baltimore
Paula Tyroler, Canada

Others donated their time:

Andre Brewster, a trustee emeritus at Johns Hopkins Hospital: Legal Issues

Charles Caviness: Fundraising Chair

Judge Charles E. Curry: Donor [116, 117]

Allen Feld: Director of Continuing Education

Janet Fetkewicz (only paid employee by 2017): Retractor Communications

Howard Fishman: Responded to callers accused by children with a copy of #616 *Resources for Families Accused by Minor Children*

Frank Kane: Director of Operations

Greg Louis: Website Manager

Zipora Roth: Research Coordinator

James Simons: Administered the newsletter's "Legal Corner"

Mothers' Roles

A government survey in 1981 found that 42.7 percent of the mothers or mother substitutes tolerated the abuse of their children.[118] In allowing the abuse to continue and receiving financial and/or social benefits in return, these mothers were effectively trafficking their children. We may try to excuse a father—perhaps he was molested as a child. We have no easy excuses for mothers who fail to protect their children.

Mothers' volunteer contributions to the Foundation were sizeable. They served as contacts for 75 percent of the state chapters[119] and half of the international groups.[120, 121]

In the HBO documentary, *Allen and Farrow*, Dylan Farrow's adoptive mother, Mia Farrow, says she dismissed many of the clues. Woody couldn't be a child molester, she thought. It wasn't until she dropped by Woody's apartment unannounced and discovered nude photos of Mia's adopted, college-age daughter, Soon-Yi, that Mia finally accepted his suspect behavior as evidence of abuse.

Polygraphs for Members

The middle-class Foundation members did not resemble the "dirty old men" we warn our children about. "We are a good-looking bunch of people, graying hair, well-dressed, healthy, smiling, with similar stories. You would want to count the members as friends," Executive Director Freyd announced in the Foundation's first newsletter.[122]

Polygraphs were suggested. "If all members of the FMS Foundation either have had or express a willingness to be polygraphed, we will have a powerful statement that we are not in the business of representing pedophiles."

The polygraph results appeared in the June 1992 newsletter. "From the survey we learned that 78% of those accused either had or were willing to take a lie-detector test. 12% told us they had already done so and one stated that he did not pass. Twenty-two percent of the respondents said they had been advised to go along with the charges and to confess in order to have contact with their children and grandchildren."[123]

The Foundation stopped suggesting polygraphs. A disclaimer followed. "We . . . are unable to judge the truth or falsity of any story that we have been told by people who call the Foundation."[124]

"It's surprising how few stories explore the question of whether accused parents are guilty or innocent," noted investigative journalist Mike Stanton, one of the few who fact-checked false memory claims. Stanton's "U-Turn on Memory Lane" appeared in the July/August 1997 issue of the *Columbia Journalism Review*.[125]

Credibility for the Foundation

> "Powerful sources have their own agendas, and when
> reporters accept what they say without question, they cross
> an ethical line. They also run the risk of being used as
> convenient vessels for the leaking of information."

—Aiden White, *Ethical Source Development*, 2016

"It is the presence of the Board that has given our efforts credibility," the Foundation announced. "Board members make substantial donations to the Foundation in both time and money."[126] Early board members included Emily and Martin Orne, MD;[127] Robyn M. Dawes, PhD; George F. Ganaway, MD; Rochel Gelman, PhD; Henry Gleitman, PhD; Lila Gleitman, PhD; Ernest Hilgard, PhD; Philip

Holzman, PhD; Ray Hyman, PhD; John Kihlstrom, PhD; Harold Lief, MD; Elizabeth Loftus, PhD; Paul McHugh, MD; Ulric Neisser, PhD; Margaret Singer, PhD; and Richard Ofshe, PhD.

Elizabeth Loftus, PhD

Psychology professor Elizabeth Loftus, PhD, played a leading role in the parents' campaign. She compared her work to those who risked their lives to save Jews. "I feel like Oskar Schindler," she told *Boston Globe* reporter J. P. Kahn in a 1994 interview.[128]

Loftus's primary contributions included (1) creating and promoting "implanted by therapists," (2) inflating the original results of her mall study to support her implanted theory, (3) altering the details of high-profile recovered memory cases to conform to the Foundation's false memory claims and (4) promoting false memories during presentations to over 300 audiences. Her TED Talk, "How Reliable Is Your Memory?" has been viewed by millions.

Loftus listed what she considers corroboration for the allegations in *CA v. Akiki* in 1993: medical evidence, pornography, videotapes, and photographs (p. 58). The Freeman case in Washington State may meet Loftus's corroboration standard. Kylie Freeman, then sixteen, recalled sexual abuse by her father as she watched *Forrest Gump* with her mother and stepfather. Kylie's father had filmed himself molesting his daughter, then he had downloaded the videos to the Internet. Kylie's mother identified the child in the videos as her daughter.[129] Kenneth Freeman pled guilty in 2008 and was sentenced to fifty years in prison. The child porn series has been viewed by millions.

Paul McHugh, MD

Before joining the Foundation's board, Johns Hopkins psychiatrist Paul McHugh supported traumatic amnesia for childhood trauma. He appeared on *Nightline* in 1990 with Richard Berendzen, a former university president. After Berendzen recalled childhood molestation by his mother, he began making obscene phone calls. McHugh explained to viewers, "Many, many individuals suffer similar kinds of consequences of early life experience during the formative age and then when this is reawakened, by a trigger of this sort, show it again."[130] McHugh changed his mind when he joined the Foundation board. "Severe traumas are not blocked out by children, but are remembered all too well," he told a *Washington Post* reporter in 1993.[131]

McHugh invited well-known academics to speak to his psychiatric trainees. He rose to vociferously disagree with any speaker who did not share his post-1990 views regarding trauma and memory. The Foundation paid McHugh's daughter and her husband over $100,000 to ghostwrite McHugh's 2008 book, *Try to Remember: Psychiatry's Clash Over Meaning, Memory, and Mind.*[132]

Other Board Members

Jon Baron, PhD, Jennifer Freyd's undergraduate mentor at the University of Pennsylvania, resigned from the board in February 1993. Ray Hyman, PhD, Jennifer's colleague at the University of Oregon, resigned in April 1993. Ralph Underwager joined the board in April 1993. He resigned from the board three months later following *Moving Forward* editor Lana Lawrence's report of Underwager's 1991 interview supporting pedophiles in *Paidika: The Journal of Pedophilia.*[133] Hollida Wakefield, his wife, remained on the board.

Underwager named reporters who would not challenge the parents' stories: Trevor Armbrister, editor of *Reader's Digest* in Washington DC; Stephanie Salter with the *San Francisco Examiner*, and Jim Okerblom with the *San Diego Union-Tribune.*[134]

The Bigger the Numbers, the Bigger the Story

> "Journalism waits until a community problem becomes 'project-sized' before reporters and editors take interest and unleash the full power of watchdog journalism."
>
> **—Stephen J. Berry, *Watchdog Journalism: The Art of Investigative Reporting*, 2008**

"It is our numbers that will let the world know how widespread this nonsense has become," the Foundation announced.[135] "Activists use statistics to persuade," they explained, "but these numbers must be understood for what they are—part of the rhetoric of social problems promotion."[136] Based on the prevalence of child sex abuse among adults,[137] the group may have been expecting a membership in the millions.

Foundation membership stood at 2,149 for the fiscal year ending February 18, 1994 (IRS Form 990, p. 2) and peaked the following year at approximately 2,573.[138] Foundation members then inflated their membership reports. "We start the new year with almost 10,000 families."[139] "We stopped publishing the numbers when they hit 10,000," Pam Freyd informed Joseph P. Kahn at *The Boston Globe* later that year.[140]

Author Lawrence Wright claimed "thousands" in "Remembering Satan" for *The New Yorker* in 1994. When psychiatrist Judith Herman asked Wright how many cases of false accusations he'd documented, Wright replied, "One."[141]

Elizabeth Loftus and Larry Cahill reported "thousands of contested cases in 2007."[142]

Board member Fredrick Crews claimed a million in "The Revenge of the Repressed, Part I" for *The New York Review of Books* in 1994.

Accused parent Mark Pendergrast topped his colleagues with his report of "several million cases" in *Victims of Memory* (p. 491). Notably, his estimate more closely reflects the prevalence of adults molested as children in the U.S.

Contributions in the Millions

Based on the Foundation's reports to the IRS, annual contributions peaked at $800,000 in 1994. The United Way granted agency status to the Foundation, and employers matched parents' donations. Contributions totaled $5.5 million at the end of their first decade. A majority of the nonprofit's expenditures are listed under "program services" described as communicating with parents, the media, and the public. Total reported expenditures stood at $7.75M when Pamela Freyd announced the Foundation's closure in December 2019 after 27 years.

As the calls and donations slowed in 2000, the group moved its office to the library of Martin Orne's Experimental Psychiatry Board and cut back to a three-day workweek. The media continued to report Foundation claims as fact until 2002 when investigative reporters uncovered cases of multi-victim child sex abuse in tolerant institutions.

What Is the False Memory Syndrome?

The Foundation was in no hurry to define their syndrome. A lengthy definition by psychologist John Kihlstrom appeared nearly 18 months later in the Foundation's August 1993 newsletter. The newsletter quoted Kihlstrom's lengthy definition in "Recovery of Memory in Laboratory and Clinic," given at the joint convention of the Rocky Mountain Psychological Association and the Western Psychological Association in Phoenix in April 1993.

> When a memory is distorted, or confabulated, the result can be what has been called the False Memory Syndrome—a condition in which a person's identity and interpersonal relationships are centered around a memory of a traumatic experience that is objectively false but in which the person strongly believes. Note that the syndrome is not characterized by false memories as such. We all have memories that are inaccurate. Rather, the syndrome may be diagnosed when the memory is so deeply ingrained that it orients the individual's entire personality and lifestyle, in turn disrupting all sorts of other adaptive behaviors. The analogy to personality disorder is intentional. False Memory Syndrome is especially destructive because the person assiduously avoids confrontation with any evidence that might challenge the memory. Thus it takes on a life of its own, encapsulated, and resistant to correction. The person may become so focused on the memory that he or she may be effectively distracted from coping with the real problems in his or her life.

"Claims about the so-called False Memory Syndrome have been diverse and influential," psychologist Ken Pope stated in his open letter to the American Psychological Association in 1995.[143] "Some involve the wholesale application of the FMS diagnosis to individuals with whom the diagnosing clinicians have had no contact." Pope is the author of several books discussing ethical considerations for the psychology profession.

The APA gave the Foundation its blessing in 1995 and approved the group as a continuing education provider for its members.[144]

The false memory story for adults' abuse accusations went viral. From 1987 through 2000, 21 articles at https://dynamic.uoregon.edu/jjf/suggestedrefs.html show that recovered memories can be corroborated.

Diagnostic Criteria for the Syndrome

David Calof, in his dual role as a clinician and editor of *Treating Abuse Today*, asked for the syndrome's diagnostic criteria. The criteria would assist the media and family members in better understanding adults' allegations.

"We have been a little horrified," Calof said, "each time Pamela Freyd has been introduced in the media as the wife of a falsely accused husband." He explained, "For the most part, these news stories have not strenuously challenged the parents' claims, nor have they reported how the daughter's accusations were made, their specific nature, or how they were proven false, if indeed they were." Calof scheduled an interview with Freyd. The interview is online.[145]

An excerpt from Part 1 of the interview in the May/June 1993 issue of *Treating Abuse Today (TAT)*:

TAT: *The cases you describe are word against word. Your basis for saying they're false memories is that the parents dispute them . . .*

Freyd: *I have said from the beginning we don't know the truth or falsity of any story . . . (p. 34)*

TAT: *But here's my issue with you not knowing. If I was talking to the executive director of the Muscular Dystrophy Association, who presumably is also not a clinician, I'll bet he or she could give me the signs and symptoms of muscular dystrophy. But in the case of false memory syndrome, so far no one seems to be able to say.*

Freyd: *So let me talk to Dr. Paul McHugh and a couple of the other people who have felt very comfortable with using false memory syndrome, and let's see if we can't pull something together that will be helpful to you" (p. 39).*

An excerpt from part 2 of the interview in the July/August 1993 issue follows. The diagnostic criteria have been modified for clarity. The original text is online as noted.

Freyd: *I spoke with several of our scientific advisory board members, and I have some information for you that isn't really in writing at this point but I think it's a direction you want us to go in, so if I can read some of these notes . . .*

TAT: *Please do.*

Freyd: *One would look for false memory syndrome*

- if a patient reports having been molested by someone in very early childhood, but then claims that she or he had complete amnesia about it for a decade or more;
- if there are firm, confident denials by the alleged perpetrators;
- if there is denial by the entire family;
- if there is no evidence that the perpetrator had alcohol dependency or bipolar disorder or tendencies to pedophilia;
- if some of the accusations are preposterous or impossible: *made pregnant prior to menarche, forced to engage in sex with animals,*[146] *or participating in the ritual killing of animals; and*
- if, in the absence of evidence of distress surrounding the putative abuse, the child displayed normal social and academic functioning.

TAT: *I take issue with several. But at least it gives us more of a sense of what you all mean when you say "false memory syndrome" (p. 27).*

However, the lack of solid diagnostic criteria for the false memory syndrome was a weak point in the parents' false memory theory. "Firm, confident denials" are not typically seen as evidence of innocence. Alcoholism and pedophilia tendencies make the accusation more likely. *The Baltimore Sun* described Peter Freyd's alcohol dependency.[147] The *Portland Oregonian* described his pedophilic tendencies.[148] Katie Heaney's "The Memory War" in *The Cut/New York Magazine* in 2021 includes a detailed overview of the Freyd family dynamics.[149] Diagnostic criteria for the syndrome are not listed on the Foundation's website or in their newsletters.

"There were several points early on when it dawned on me that the False Memory Syndrome (FMS) Foundation was a political advocacy group masquerading as a scientifically-oriented foundation," Calof said in an interview. "The final straw was when I interviewed Pamela Freyd for *Treating Abuse Today*. Like Loftus, she did not evince any kind of scientific curiosity about trauma and dissociation or about therapeutic influence." He added, "They turned the scientific model on its head by starting with certainty about a conclusion (adults' accusations are false) and then cherry-picking data to substantiate it."

Jennifer Freyd and FMS Criteria

Psychology professor Jennifer Freyd spoke publicly about her family for the first time at a conference in 1993. The media portrayed her parents as falsely accused, she told the audience. She quoted Wendy Schmelzer's introduction of her mother on NPR's *All Things Considered*. "Dr. (Pamela) Freyd has crisscrossed the country with the same message—you are not alone. My husband and I were also falsely accused."

She described her father's alcohol dependency and some of his pedophilic tendencies. She read aloud a troubling poem she had written at thirteen. Her sister and her paternal uncle supported her allegations, she said. Jennifer dismissed Pamela's "Jane Doe" article as inaccurate and defaming. Explaining her decision to cease contact with her parents, she said, "I made the decision to protect myself from continued sexualized discussions, continued blaming, and continued denial only after repeated attempts to make the communication work."[150]

Pamela responded by once more gaslighting Jennifer. "More than 200 therapists stood and cheered as one of the speakers denounced her parents," she said. "Putting aside the truth or falsity of the abuse allegations because that is not an appropriate topic for this newsletter . . . What if the story were not quite right and the denouncer was disturbed?"[151]

Pennsylvania, Home of the FMS Foundation

Executive Director Pamela Freyd testified in 1994 against extending the statute of limitations for lawsuits in Pennsylvania. To do so "may create more tarnished reputations," she suggested.[152]

Until 2003, the twelve-hour training for Child Protective Services (CPS) workers in Pennsylvania included two thirty-minute segments (Sections 11-D, and III-E) featuring fourteen untested indicators of "knowingly false" reports.[153] The presence of just one indicator meant that an allegation could be ruled "knowingly false" and dismissed by the caseworker. Indicators included items such as "alleged perpetrators claim that the allegations are false," and "undertones of retaliation or revenge." Contacted in 2003, CPS administrators agreed to drop these sections. CPS in Pennsylvania was verifying 10.8 percent of child abuse reports compared to the US average of 16.9 percent.

A Pennsylvania Grand Jury report in 2018 found the Catholic Church had protected 300 abusive priests.

The Pennsylvania governor approved legislation in 2019, ending time limits for police to file criminal charges and allowing victims of childhood crimes more time to file lawsuits.

SIRS Books

Foundation members Elliott and Eleanor Goldstein with Social Issues Resources Series Publishing (SIRS) released three books supporting false memory claims. *Confabulations: Creating False Memories, Destroying Families* was distributed to the media in 1992. A *Library Journal* reviewer expressed skepticism about the next SIRS book,

True Stories of False Memories. "Most of the evidence purporting to demonstrate that 'an epidemic of false accusations is occurring' is anecdotal and one-sided, culled from more than 500 responses to an 800 telephone number," she wrote.[154] The final book, *Smiling Through Tears*, by Goldstein and Pamela Freyd in 1998, features dozens of cartoons depicting the media's skeptical attitude toward victims and therapists.

Repressed or Always Remembered—Does It Matter?

The Foundation's campaign focused on repressed memories, a less likely circumstance than incidents that were always remembered. If the adult had always remembered, parents typically created a false memory version of the accusation. Linda McEwen is a retired tax professional. Her mother, Pat Knight, was one of the leaders of the Indiana Friends of FMSF chapter, later named the Indiana Association for Responsible Mental Health Practices.

McEwen explains, "I always remembered the molestation. My father molested me when I was a teenager." McEwen speaks for many when she says, "No one believed me years later when I confronted my father about this crime. Once I was aware of the False Memory Syndrome Foundation and my parents' membership in it, I knew it didn't matter if my memories of incest were repressed or always remembered."

Her parents created a history for her that fit the false memory narrative, Linda says, complete with a therapist who supposedly convinced her that she had been molested. "No therapist had to convince me," she explains, "because I'd always remembered. When I consulted an attorney, it was the statute of limitations that silenced me, not the characteristics of my memories."[155]

Does Sexual Contact With an Adult Harm a Child?

False memory advocates stand firm in their belief that having to perform sexual activities with a parent or other trusted adult does not harm a child.[156] The Adverse Child Experience (ACE) study is "sloppy science," they said.[157]

Psychologist and future APA President Martin Seligman chaired a panel at the Foundation's first conference. In his book, *What You Can Change and What You Can't*, Seligman suggests that the body of work suggesting sexual abuse results in harm is "lacking methodological niceties" (p. 233).

Psychologist Elizabeth Loftus blamed any mental health difficulties on unspecified family dysfunction. Speaking at a conference in 1994, she said that "variables are reduced to nothing" once family dysfunction is factored out (p. 27).[158]

"For some people, it may not be traumatic," Pamela Freyd suggested in her interview with David Calof for *Treating Abuse Today*.

Canadian attorney Alan Gold asked, "How much of the aftermath is that they are being told they are destroyed?" (p. 24).

James Hudson, MD, maintained, "The premise that childhood sexual abuse can precipitate adult mental-health difficulties is without scientific foundation. Bad genetics will turn out to be the culprit" (p. 27).

Accused parent Mark Pendergrast in *Victims of Memory* says, "Sexually abused children, fondled by an otherwise nurturing family member, do not always experience the incident as abusive, and some children are not traumatized by an adult's sexual attentions."[159]

Psychologist Susan Clancy in *The Trauma Myth* suggests that, since child molestation is not typically violent, then it is not typically traumatic. She failed to cite Clancy & McNally (2005/2006, p. 69) in which survivors rated the trauma they experienced at 7.5 on a 10-point trauma scale.

In Mary Wright's documentary "Am I Crazy?" SIRS publisher and FMS Foundation member Eleanor Goldstein reports, "I don't think sexual touch is the horror of all horrors. I don't think so. I think we make a big to-do about nothing."[160]

Foundation board member and law professor Ralph Slovenko "railed against the laws that held offenders accountable for sex with a child."[161]

Board member Hollida Wakefield said in a *Paedika* interview, "The climate is such in the United States [it's considered a crime] that it would be very, very, very, very difficult for a pedophile, even with the most idealistic of motives and aspirations, to make his [sexual] relationship [with a child] work in practice."[162]

"Children are naturally sexual and may initiate sexual encounters by 'seducing' the adult," Richard Gardner, MD, maintained in 1986.[163] Gardner's *True and False Accusations of Child Sex Abuse* is "valuable for scholarly understanding and insights" the Foundation told its members.[164] A tape of Gardner's September 1993 presentation to FMSF members was available for $15.[165]

ANSWER: Sexual contact with an adult harms a child.

The Adverse Child Experience (ACE) study focuses on the impact of emotional, physical, and/or sexual abuse experienced by a child before age eighteen. The CDC–Kaiser Adverse Child Experience (ACE) Study in 1998 of 17,337 adults is cited in 9,400 Google Scholar articles and is widely accepted in the academic, medical, and governmental health communities. The study found that 20.7 percent of the adult patients surveyed stated they were molested as children.[166]

Post-traumatic stress disorder (PTSD), a common result following childhood trauma, is associated with accelerated aging and illnesses in which immune activation has a key role, such as cardiovascular diseases and diabetes.[167] Per victim estimates of the lifetime cost of non-fatal child maltreatment begin at $210,000.[168] These costs are typically covered by the victim and society.

Two CDC studies found that amnesia is a common result for children who experience trauma. A study in 2001, "Autobiographical Memory Disturbances in Childhood Abuse Survivors," found that a history of childhood physical or sexual abuse doubled the prevalence of autobiographical memory loss for women. For men, the rate was 1.5 times that of men with no abuse history. A CDC study in 2007, "Adverse Childhood Experiences and Childhood Autobiographical Memory Disturbance," found that, as a person's ACE score increased, the prevalence of amnesia increased.

Chapter 12

Marketing False Memories

"We can hardly trumpet our role as important watchdogs
of the public interest unless we are willing to follow the
story through and determine if the public's interest is being
adequately safeguarded. If we fail at this, we are nothing
but scandalmongers."

**—Madelaine Drohan, *Nieman Report*, "Knowing When to
Stop Reporting about a Scandal," 2005**

The decade of reckoning with child molesters in the 1980s was
over.[169] The false memory campaign of the 1990s resembled the
well-funded cigarette manufacturers' campaign of the 1950s. When
nearly half of the U.S. population smoked,[170] researchers found
smoking-related links to cancer. In response, the tobacco industry
spent millions disseminating a "No cancer link to tobacco" message
that smokers wanted to believe. Surveys showed that 20 percent of
adults are molested as children and legislatures allowed them to sue
for damages. In response, accused parents spent millions disseminating a "the accusations are false memories" message the public likely
wanted to believe.

Six cigarette companies formed the Tobacco Industry Research
Committee, backed by an advisory board of credentialed experts.
Accused parents established the False Memory Syndrome Founda-
tion backed by an advisory board of credentialed experts.

The media called the tobacco industry's disinformation campaign, "The Great Debate." They called the False Memory Syndrome Foundation's disinformation campaign, "The Memory Wars."

Tobacco manufacturers' insisted the media present a "balanced" response by quoting industry spokespeople saying cancer may be related to other causes. The FMS Foundation did the same, insisting the media quote their credentialed board members who said the accusations might be false memories.

Once the public accepted that smoking is related to health problems, the smoking population fell from 45 percent to 14 percent by 2018. Once the false memory story went viral, fewer child sex cases were reported.

Introducing False Memories to the Media

"The concern that young victims are prone to suggestibility
pales in comparison to the suggestibility of grown and
experienced newspapermen."

—Judge Simons, *Berkshire Eagle,* 2003

Like the cigarette manufacturers' campaign, the false memory campaign is a blend of truth, lies, and beliefs. The Foundation's early media success rested on contacting reporters who would not question their evidence—the story of an older brother who convinced his younger brother he was lost. There was no press conference introducing the parents as falsely accused. Such an event might have raised questions regarding the parents' motives. Instead, University of Washington memory researcher Elizabeth Loftus, PhD, approached individual reporters.

A key detail was missing from the story the public heard—Coan implied he was present when his brother supposedly got lost. However, a therapist could not tell a client they were present when the client was molested.

Dan Goleman's "Childhood Trauma: Memory or Invention?"[171] for *The New York Times* introduced false memories in July 1992. He called the Coan story "a pertinent experiment on the malleability of human memory." He told readers about the False Memory Syndrome Foundation in Philadelphia.

The Associated Press followed in August, sending *Seattle Times* reporter Bill Dietrich's story to newsrooms across the country. The headline established a new copyediting standard—sneer quotes around "repressed," suggesting disbelief: "UW Expert Challenges 'Repressed' Memories—Says Some Sexual Abuse May Not Be Real."[172] Like Goleman, Dietrich presented the story as a debate among experts. He told readers, incorrectly, that false memories were implanted in Loftus's first five mall study subjects—the study had not yet been approved. Dietrich failed to tell readers that adults who had always remembered the abuse could also sue for damages.

Dietrich led with, "Repressed memories of sexual abuse may be false and can be inadvertently suggested by therapists, University of Washington psychologist Elizabeth Loftus will tell the American Psychological Association (APA) tomorrow."

Researchers generally do not mock their research participants. However, Loftus mocked the spelling errors in Coan's mother's response as she read it aloud during her APA presentation, "I've tried and tried to rember this day I see, uh, looking under clothes racks for Christopher's feet, but I can't honestly say that was the time. I do not rember this. I do not rember (laughter)."[173]

Loftus told her audience, "It's still a step away from getting someone to believe that they were lost in a shopping mall at the age of five and that they were crying and rescued and so on to developing memories of abuse." The media took that step.

The False Memory Media Phenomenon

"Why is it that we're wary of victims making false accusations, but rarely consider how many men have lied about, downplayed, or manipulated others to cover their own actions."

—Chanel Miller, *Know My Name*, 2019

The more often we hear a story, the more likely we are to believe it.[174] By 1995, the parents' false memory story had found a home in the popular press. Over 300 articles—one every three to four days—reported the false memory claims. Many advised their friends and family members their memories of abuse were false. They knew this was true because they'd read about it. Adults molested as children were silenced. They would remain so until they could speak out on social media. Many therapists would sit quietly on the sidelines, afraid of being sued if a client reported they were molested. Research supporting the claims of victims was published in scholarly journals, unseen by the popular press.

The cover statement for the Foundation's first media packet in June 1992 shifted the story from family members molesting children to therapists causing family suffering:

The False Memory Syndrome Phenomenon

"While our awareness of childhood sexual abuse has increased enormously in the last decade and the horrors of its consequences should never be minimized, there is another side to this situation, namely that of the consequences of false allegations where whole families are split apart and terrible pain inflicted on everyone concerned. This side of the story needs to be told, for a therapist may, with the best intentions in the world, contribute to enormous family suffering."

—Harold Lief, MD; Emeritus Professor of Psychiatry, University of Pennsylvania, November 1991

FMS Foundation
False Memory Syndrome

3508 Market Street—Suite 128—Philadelphia, PA 19104—215-387-1865 — 800-568-8882.

This collection of articles was compiled by the False Memory Syndrome Foundation to explore some of the questions that arise when adults claim to have recovered long-repressed memories of childhood abuse.

The Foundation invested $500,000 in postage during the early 1990s as they distributed their false memory story to reporters, textbook editors, attorneys, academics, clinicians, and health care providers.

Anita Creamer with *The Sacramento Bee* told readers, "The False Memory Syndrome Foundation sends me newsletters and press releases designed to debunk the notion that long-repressed memories of abuse and incest—recovered memories—can surface in adulthood and should be taken seriously."

"Much of the material I have received from the False Memory Syndrome Foundation scares me," *Seattle Times* columnist Jennifer James said in her November 19, 1995, column. "They are so sure they are right—always right—about what is a very complex element in human behavior and awareness."

Margot Forrest described the campaign's impact on survivors. "With FMSF leading the charge, a backlash developed that was so effective and powerful, survivors began to retreat into historical muteness," she reported in her *Healing Woman* newsletter. "Our subscriber numbers began to drop. Fewer women were 'coming out of the closet.' Fewer therapists were willing to see survivors, due to the lawsuits that could ensue."

Foundation members approached reporters individually. Steve Elbow's "Rethinking the 'False Memory' Controversy" in 2011 described one member's approach. "A Wisconsin member of the Foundation gave me a call to tip me off to a case," he said, "then put me in contact with executive director Pamela Freyd, who offered compelling quotes and easy research for a reporter trying to cobble together a quick and interesting story." Elbow says, "It never occurred to me that I was dealing with a highly organized public-relations machine until a victim and a sexual-assault advocate emailed me with their concerns."[175]

The public saw only the headline stories. They were unaware that accused child molesters were spending millions on a PR campaign to ensure the public believed the repeated stories.

Quote Slants, Story Ledes, and Rhetoric

"Journalists have long gathered expert quotes, secretly hoping to have our angles confirmed and our fears of imposture put to rest."

—Alisa Quart, *Columbia Journalism Review*, 2010

The expert quote serves as the voice of reason, ridding us of any doubts we might have regarding what the author has said. Researchers Ross E. Cheit, Yael Shavit, and Zachary Reiss-Davis introduced "quote slant" as a measure of determining whether a reporter has slanted an article.[176] The opinion of the majority of experts quoted by the reporter reflects the reporter's own belief about a subject.

Quote slants for the articles in the Foundation's first press packet indicate early media support for child sex abuse claims as false. Expert quotes supporting accused individuals are identified as "A." Pro-victim quotes are identified as "V."

1. *"Childhood Trauma: Memory or Invention?" by Daniel Goleman, The New York Times, (4A/2V)*

2. *"Unlocking the Secrets of Memory" by Irene Wielawski, Los Angeles Times, (4A/1V)*

3. *"When Can Memories Be Trusted?" by Anastasia Toufexis, TIME, (4A/1V)*

4–7. *Four columns by Darrell Sifford, The Philadelphia Inquirer, (7A/0V)*

8. *"Abuse of Trust" by Glenna Whitley, D Magazine (no experts, just ex-patients all claiming false memories)*

9–11. *Three articles by Bill Taylor, Toronto Star, (6A/1V)*

12. *"Satanism: Truth vs. Myth" by Jim Okerblom, San Diego Union-Tribune, (3A/0V)*

13. *"Investigator's Guide to Allegations of 'Ritual' Child Abuse" by Kenneth V. Lanning, FBI (no expert quotes)*

14. *"Scientific Status of Refreshing Recollection by the Use of Hypnosis" by the Council on Scientific Affairs in the Journal of American Medical Association, 1985 (no expert quotes).*

TOTAL: Pro-accused: 28, Pro-victim: 5

False Memory Ledes

A "lede" is the opening sentence or paragraph of a news article emphasizing what the reporter believes is the most important aspect(s) of the story.[177] Bill Taylor with the *Toronto Star* set the standard for anonymous false memory ledes with, "There is anguish in John Brown's eyes but his voice is steady. 'I did not beat my daughter. I did not molest my daughter' . . . John and Jean Brown (not their real names) are among a growing number of parents across North America who are denying accusations."

False Memory Rhetoric

Readers' beliefs can be swayed by whether the author frames the accuser or the accused as the victim.[178] The Foundation's media campaign relied on "victim framing," a rhetorical device that casts the accused parents as the "real" victims. Mark Sauer and Jim Okerblom's two-part series, "Haunting Accusations: Repressed Memories of Childhood Abuse; Real or Delusions?" for the *San Diego Union-Tribune* in August 1992 reads like a thesaurus for rhetoric that the national press would soon echo. Like all successful rhetoric, the ideas are simple and emotionally arousing.

1. *"Misguided therapists use hypnosis and visualization to generate memories."*

2. *"The accusations are absurd, incredible, impossible, extreme."*

3. *"The accuser is seriously ill/disturbed/confused."*

4. *"Clients are highly suggestible and/or highly hypnotizable."*

5. *"There's an epidemic of false memories."*

6. *"There's growing sex abuse hysteria."*

7. *"Repressed memory therapy is devastating families."*

8. *"Experts challenge repressed memories."*

9. *"Sexual abuse is a serious problem, but so are false accusations."*

10. *"Repressed memories divert attention from real abuse."*

11. *"Clients with everyday problems look for explanations."*

12. *"Memory is malleable, not like a videotape."*

Statements 1–4 are name-calling directed at an individual, rather than at the position they support. Statements 5 and 6 are exaggerations for effect. "Epidemic" and "growing hysteria" are emotionally arousing terms, meaningless without supporting data.

Statement (7) incorrectly suggests this is an actual therapy approach. The addition of "devastating families" lends an emotional appeal. (8) Citing anonymous experts who challenge repressed memories lends further credibility.

Statement 9 is "chaining." The first half is relatively uncontroversial. Readers who agree with the first half are more likely to agree with what follows. Statement 10 suggests that, without the distraction of repressed memories, we would pay attention to always-remembered abuse. Perhaps. Statement 11 suggests that everyday problems that interfere with clients' daily lives draw them to therapy.

The most often repeated claim (12) is arguable. The term originated in 1937 with Wilder Penfield, MD, a Canadian brain surgeon. Penfield stimulated various parts of the brain with electrodes during surgery for intractable epilepsy. He found that stimulating the temporal lobe and the hippocampus caused patients to recall long-forgotten experiences.[179]

I tested the effectiveness of these persuasive techniques with a local Toastmasters group. I distributed a list of techniques.[180] We briefly discussed each one. I described Loftus to them as a memory expert. Then I asked them to watch a five-minute video segment of one of her presentations. I'd already watched the segment and counted seven persuasive techniques. How many would they identify, I wondered. We watched the film, and I asked, "Did you see her use any persuasive techniques?" The room was silent. I ran the tape again and pointed out each technique and explained it. "Rhetoric is effective because it slips in under our radar," I told them.

Accused Parents As Sources

A new source went public in the 1990s—parents accused of incest telling dramatic stories of families torn apart by false accusations. Mark Sauer and Jim Okerblom with the *San Diego Union-Tribune* established a reporting model—interview the accused parent, not the accuser. They told readers, "Contacted at their apartment, Jane and Mark's daughter-in-law said she and her husband (B. C.) would not talk" (p. D-3).

"One of the reporters knocked on our front door a few weeks before the first article came out," B. C. said in an interview. "My wife told him I wasn't home. That was the last we heard from him. The 'Mark and Jane C.' from Palmdale in the article are my parents. The reporters drove over two hours to interview them. I guess that's the story they wanted to tell."

B. C.'s letter to the *Union-Tribune* corrected the errors in the article. The letter was not published. B. C. said he received a response from a *Union-Tribune* staff member saying if B. C. believed he experienced a ritualized form of abuse as a child, then he was crazy (personal communication; July 9, 2010).

Okerblom works in public relations with Cubic Corporation San Diego. Sauer left KPBS in 2021.

Blame the Books

The release of *The Courage to Heal: A Guide for Women Survivors of Child Sexual Abuse* in 1988 coincided with the passage of the first state law in Washington allowing adults molested as children to sue for damages. Authors Ellen Bass and Laura Davis said they wanted their title to reflect the courage and commitment required by a decision to undertake the healing journey. More than 200 sources, primarily students in the authors' writing classes and support groups, contributed their personal experiences to the book.[181]

The first three years of the Foundation's newsletters included nearly 100 negative comments regarding *Courage*. The parents focused on one sentence: "If you think you were abused and your life shows the symptoms, then you were" (p. 22).[182] To date, no study has found that reading that sentence or any other sentence in *Courage* has convinced someone that he or she was molested. Memory researcher Elizabeth Loftus testified in *Crook v. M.* that she did not recover any memories of abuse after reading the book (pp. 36–37).

The media quoted the Foundation's claims about the book as fact, rather than fact-checking the Foundation's claims. "I tried every approach I could think of—humor, research, tragic stories—to get the recovered memory story across to reporters," Bass said in an interview. "Nothing worked. Reporters seemed intent on one story—false memories."[183]

HarperCollins released the fourth edition of The Courage to Heal on the book's twentieth anniversary. Book sales average 10,000–12,000 annually, not including foreign sales or *The Courage to Heal Workbook* sales. Lawsuits filed against the authors claiming that reading the book had implanted false memories were dismissed.

Author Barbara Graham said she was asked to do a story on recovered memories for *Redbook*. To prepare for the assignment, she read E. Sue Blume's *Secret Survivors*. Graham's "Unlock the Secrets of Your Past," in January 1993 lacked the false memory rhetoric typical of the time. Blume's book, Graham said, helped her better understand the abusive relationship with a camp counselor she had experienced as a teen. She wrote about the relationship in "Swept Out of My Childhood into a Nameless Sea."[184]

Accused parents in Texas attempted to have the self-help books for survivors declared pornographic. They asked the state attorney general and the Department of Health and Human Services to investigate several books including *The Courage to Heal*.[185] "Every description is of deviant sex," the parents claimed. The books were not determined to be pornographic.

The Myth of Repressed Memories by Elizabeth Loftus and Katherine Ketcham was released in September 1994, following the failure of the mall study in mid-1994. Loftus assigned the book as required reading for her psychology classes at the University of Washington.

Readers Beware

"Beware the Incest-Survivor Machine" by Carol Tavris appeared in *The New York Times Book Review* (NYTBR) on January 3, 1993, and in the Foundation's January newsletter. "The problem is not with the advice [the books] offer to victims," Tavris explained, "but with their effort to create victims to expand the market that can then be treated with therapy and self-help books."[186]

Readers responded.[187] Judith Lewis Herman, MD, author of *Trauma and Recovery*, wrote, "Books on incest are so popular because there are so many victims . . . If Ms. Tavris is really so tired of hearing about incest, she should stop trashing other women and join with us to try and end the epidemic of sexual violence."

"Despite Ms. Tavris's argument that *Secret Survivors* presents groundless theories unsupported by research, my conclusions are compiled from field observation and extensive interviews with survivors, and are supported by many studies," E. Sue Blume wrote.

Ellen Bass and Laura Davis responded, "Carol Tavris condemns our book, *The Courage to Heal*, and the incest-survivor movement in general. We'd like to respond to her criticisms." They did.

"Ms. Tavris's assertion that I 'never actually remembered' being abused by my father puzzles me since one of the themes of my memoir is the very process of remembering what happened," said Betsy Peterson, author of *Dancing with Daddy*.

English professor Ceil Malek noted, "Ms. Tavris rightly questions the absence of empirical evidence to support assertions in some of the popular books on incest . . . However, Ms. Tavris could also be accused of having no real evidence that women are inappropriately being coaxed into an 'incest-survivor machine' or that significant numbers of unethical therapists are luring women into remembering incest that did not occur."

Tavris responded, "I fear that the current sad and destructive impulse to see abuse in every home and to manufacture memories where none existed, is creating a dangerous new set of problems."

Parents' Campaign Activities

"When you are at the center of a story that the American media is paying an enormous amount of attention to, your appreciation for just how willing and eager they are to disseminate falsehoods escalates substantially."

—Glen Greenwald, "The Surveillance State," 2017

The Foundation newsletter's "What Can Families Do?" column reported that some members had picketed a therapist's office. Others were put in touch with members from the same state to explore legal options together. Surveys gathered data about specific therapists. Ethics complaints should be checked by an attorney if future legal action was intended. Meetings with therapists were "disastrous," members were advised.[188]

Freyd commended the members. "You have written letters to papers; you have knocked on politicians' doors; you have filed complaints; you have appeared in public; you have written journal articles; you have even picketed; you have kept us informed. You are changing the climate. Keep it up. We will do our part from the office, but the ending depends on you" (October 1992).

Along with their financial contributions, Foundation members were asked to

- Post an ad on local notice boards
- Help ship information packets to the deans of schools of social work, the heads of the psychological associations in each state, and the chairs of psychology departments.
- Ask to have the false-memory side of a story told
- Submit false memory narratives to *Confabulations: Creating False Memories, Destroying Families*
- Distribute Foundation pamphlets in churches, at family gatherings, in schools, to hospital patients, and in the waiting rooms of health-care providers[189]
- Follow their child to the therapist's office, hire a private

detective, pry the information from other relatives their child may talk to, pose as a patient.[190]

- Organize seminars and invite local lawyers, therapists, law enforcement, politicians, and educators to speak about solving our FMS problems as members did in MA, NY, OH, MI, AZ, PA, and VI.

- Pressure licensing boards to hear your stories by attending their meetings, telephoning them, writing letters, and "buttonholing" board members in hallways.

The California Board of Behavior Science agreed to put "repressed memory" on a meeting agenda in November 1994, members were told. Ten families spoke. The board agreed to devote a day to the subject at their February 1995 meeting.[191]

Targeting Large Audiences

The more widespread a piece of misinformation, the harder it becomes to debunk. "False memories" as the new label for crimes allegedly committed years earlier against millions of children was an easy sell in the early 1990s. Few want to hear the shocking details of what child molesters do to children, much less learn the crime was committed by someone they know. Reporters wanted a piece of this story following the Foundation's first conference in 1993.

1993 Conference

The Foundation recruited thirty-four media representatives for its first annual conference at Valley Forge in April 1993. Six hundred attendees met representatives of ABC, CBS, Fox, NBC News, CBC TV, *The New Yorker*, *The Philadelphia Inquirer*, *Psychology Today*, *San Diego Union-Tribune*, *Family Therapy Networker*, *Blue Sky Productions*, *Answers in Action Journal*, *Changes Magazine*, *Insight Magazine*, *Moving Forward*, and *Mother Jones*.

The agenda included future American Psychological Association president Martin Seligman chairing a panel of prominent Foundation board members. Judge Lisa Richette from Philadelphia chaired

"What Do Lawyers Need?" Judge Phyllis W. Beck from the Superior Court of Pennsylvania chaired "Did the Crime Occur?"

Paul McHugh, Martin Orne, Hollida Wakefield, and executive director Pam Freyd selected conference papers for distribution to college students.[192]

The Foundation's early campaign was getting the word out. The October 1993 newsletter cited false memory articles in *Newsweek*, *The Washington Post* (three articles), *USA Today*, *Rocky Mountain News*, *Mankato Free Press*, *Tribune-Review of Western PA*, and the *Arkansas Times*. *TIME*'s November 29 issue announced, "Repressed-Memory Therapy: Lies of the Mind Repressed-Memory Therapy Is Harming Patients, Devastating Families, and Intensifying a Backlash against Mental-Health Practitioners."[193]

The *U.S. News & World Report* did not cover that story. "Memories Lost and Found" by Miriam Horn described Brown University Professor Ross Cheit's experience of molestation by an administrator of the San Francisco Boys Choir summer camp.[194] Horn quoted both false-memory and traumatic amnesia experts and described Cheit's investigation of the Chorus and its summer camp administrator.

1994 Conference

Thirty reporters traveled to Baltimore in December 1994 for the Foundation's second annual conference, which was co-sponsored by the Johns Hopkins Medical Institutions. Letters to Johns Hopkins expressing concerns about the conference are stored in the FMS Foundation's archive in Buffalo, New York.

An anecdotal account in the December issue of the *Johns Hopkins University Gazette* featured Johns Hopkins psychiatrist and Foundation board member Paul McHugh, MD.[195] An unnamed retired naval officer was headed for criminal court when McHugh was called in as an expert. The unnamed parents obtained their daughter's childhood diary in which she reportedly said she was not molested and had watched the movie, *Sybil*. The case was dismissed. McHugh described the recovered memories of adults as "a craze, similar to the Red Scare, to the pogroms, to the witch trials."

The press regularly covered Foundation's annual conferences until 2002 when *The Boston Globe* broke the story of Catholic priests who were transferred to another diocese after being accused of molesting children.

The American Association of Retired People (AARP)

Members were asked to contact Teresa Varner, director of public policy, and request a story on false accusations.[196] *The AARP Bulletin* responded four months later with "Shadow Side of Memory." Staff writer Robert P. Hey described a legal strategy used by Jack Collier in Santa Cruz who was sued by his daughter. Collier's daughter had initially expressed doubts about her memories in her diary. Collier's attorney, Tom Griffin, subpoenaed the diary and read aloud excerpts questioning her early memories. "The jury returned a not-liable verdict," Hey said.

An *AARP Bulletin* communications staff person informed us the article was not available. A local librarian obtained the article.

Advice Columnists

An *Ask Ann Landers* column in October 1993, "Molestation Victims Need to Speak Out," received a flood of critical letters from Foundation members. Landers responded on December 12, describing abuse accusations as character assassinations. "By the time the facts are made public," Landers wrote, "the accused parent is thoroughly discredited and his reputation is in shreds." Landers included contact information for the Foundation.

"This is a subject about which I do not need to consult any mental health professionals. I have been receiving letters from both the abused and the abusers for as long as I've been writing this column," Landers said in a March 16, 1994, column.

A May column included letters from adults molested as children. Landers closed the column with a letter from accused parents in Missouri thanking Landers for telling them about the Foundation. Landers wasn't done. "Uncovering Memories May Lead to Problems" in a 1995 column included more letters from parents and contact information for the Foundation.

Dear Abby did not respond to parents' requests for a column on false memories. The Foundation told parents, "Although she has informed us that a letter mentioning the Foundation is on permanent hold, she is aware of the existence of the problem and the Foundation. Your letters are having results. Please keep writing to the media."[197]

Phil Donahue

"If the [November 1993] newsletter is a few days late this month, it's because of the avalanche of calls resulting from a moving *Donahue* show this week featuring three retractors and two of their mothers." The *Donahue* video was shown at an FMS seminar in Dallas the following year.

Dr. Laura

Laura Schlessinger (Dr. Laura) commented positively on her contact with a Foundation member. Her mention "brought a small deluge of telephone calls from desperate families looking for help" the July/August 1999 newsletter reported.

Presuming to Know the Truth

Media coverage of adults' childhood sex abuse allegations resembled a one-sided political campaign by 1994—the allegations were false. Psychiatrist Judith Herman's "Presuming to Know the Truth" for the *Nieman Report*[198] described how reporters covering the false memory story relied on anecdotes, speculations, and opinions of a small group of experts (p. 44). Herman listed three undocumented propositions the media had accepted as fact:

1. false claims are common,
2. claims based on delayed recall are especially likely to be spurious, and
3. fictitious memories have been instilled "wholesale in a gullible populace by quack psychotherapists."

"They [the parents] resort to war by public diplomacy," Randolph Ryan at *The Boston Globe* told Herman. They get their "falsely accused" message out to the public using in-person meetings with local press, media interviews, and the Internet.

Stephen Fried with *Philadelphia Magazine* explained how parents' influenced the media coverage. "If you've got a crying mom, you've got a story. If you've got a crying dad, my God, you've got two stories. If you don't get the other side of the story, you've got to be swayed."

Newsweek's "You Must Remember This" was typical of the time.[199] Sharon Begley led her story with the Coan brothers' anecdote describing an older brother convincing his younger brother that he was lost at a mall. She quoted four false memory proponents: Elizabeth Loftus, Daniel Schacter, Stephen Ceci, and Richard Ofshe. Begley quoted one trauma expert, psychiatrist Judith Herman, who said, "We have no way of judging independently childhood experiences as false."

"That's OK if memories are used solely in therapy, and treated as mere expressions of the mind," Begley responded. "But 'memories' are sending people to jail." Notably, memories of long-ago child sexual abuse would not send anyone to jail in most states due to the statute of limitations.

According to the National Child Abuse and Neglect Data System (NCANDS), substantiated cases of child sexual abuse declined by 62 percent between 1992, when the FMSF began its campaign, and 2010.

Chapter 13

Journalists As False Memory Advocates

"When a decision is influenced by 'gut feeling,' it's wise to explore how your unconscious bias might have led to your decision."

—Paul Cheung, *The Investigative Reporters and Editors Journal,* **2016**

"Take a stand, sure, but do so in a measured and direct way, so that your reporting speaks for itself—loudly and clearly, but not in the tone of an angry commentator."

—Michael Specter, "On the Side of Facts," *Colombia Journalism Review,* **Spring 2020**

The task for accused child molesters and their experts was to convince the media and the public that the accusations were false. The task for the media was to produce a balanced story by fact-checking the claims and digging deeper. The Foundation's early investment of $2.3M in promotion efforts through 1995 proved worthwhile. Reporters did not fact-check the parents' story. Instead, they took notes and followed leads offered by the Foundation. Hundreds of articles in the popular press portrayed adults' accusations as false memories: ninety-three in 1993, one hundred and twenty in 1994 and eighty-nine in 1995—one article every three to four days for three years.[200] Parents described as "claiming to be falsely accused" the first year became "falsely accused" by the second year. Parents' "We're falsely accused" claims became truth for the press and the public.

The *San Francisco Examiner*

"It comes down to who the editor is friends with. If he knows a victim he will do a pro-victim story. If he's friends with an accused parent he will do a pro-FMSF story.

—Stephen Freid, *Philadelphia Magazine*, interview with Judith Herman for "Ethics on Trial," 1994

"I began to look for answers," said Stephanie Salter with the *San Francisco Examiner* when her boyfriend's daughter accused him of sex abuse. Salter said she found her answer in a *New York Times* article by Daniel Goleman. She contacted the parents' group that Goleman mentioned and was put in contact with several accused parents in her area. She listened, she said, as middle-class parents— some weeping, some angry, some still in shock—told their stories.[201] Rather than examining her own interest in the story, Salter decided, "This was an important story, and my newspaper had to do it."[202]

"Buried Memories, Broken Families" by Salter and Carol Ness became a front-page, six-part series. The authors listed similarities in the parents' stories: (1) accusations follow a period of remoteness, (2) parents are cut off after the confrontation, and (3) therapists refused to meet with clients' parents.

Salter said she believed the parents. She explained, "If in all these years I can't tell who's lying . . . I have to trust what got me here over the last 20 years."

The series concluded with a letter to the editor. "Salter would have a very big stake in proving to herself that repressed memories are false. Her close companion of several years had been accused nine months earlier by his daughter. We are that daughter and her husband." The letter writers asked, "Please bring balance to this series by giving the same amount of attention to cases of repressed memories of sexual abuse that have been substantiated."

Instead, the *Examiner* followed with Salter and Ness's "Therapists Split." Four of the experts said the accusations were false memories; two said they were the result of childhood trauma.

Salter's "Feminist Treason and Intellectual Fascism" in April 1993 described Carol Tavris as criticizing "the dangerously sloppy thinking" of authors of incest survivor literature.[203] Those who agreed with Salter and Tavris have "prodigious minds and . . . noble hearts," Salter said, naming Janice Hakken, Elizabeth Loftus, Wendy Kaminer, Debbie Nathan, Carol Ness, and Carol Tavris.

Salter retired as a columnist with the *Tribune-Star* in Indiana.

Ness's articles have appeared in the *Berkleyan*, a weekly email newsletter at UC Berkeley.

KRON-TV and *Media File*

Euna Kwon at KRON-TV covered the rape of writer Caryn Stardancer. She told viewers that a therapist helped trigger Stardancer's memories.

Stardancer responded with a letter correcting the errors in Kwon's story. She was not in therapy when her memories of the rape resurfaced. She had medical records documenting the rape. She had researched the assailant's history and found he had served a prison term for raping a thirteen-year-old girl, a fact Kwon failed to mention.

Kerry Lauerman, then with the investigative publication, *Media File*, asked Kwon why she revised the facts of the rape case.

Kwon insisted that "she had to put the segment together under tight time constraints, and therefore included what she felt was most important." She added, "That's my prerogative, to edit the story. Were we to include her whole story, we would have needed 30 seconds. That's a lot of time when you have to tell the whole story in a minute and 30 seconds."[204]

Kwon serves in Surety Communications at Crum & Forster Insurance.

Lauerman is the executive news editor at *Forbes*.

Washington State Bar News

"The best advertising I do is write an article for a publication like the

American Bar Journal, which reaches 200,000 lawyers," Loftus says. "That's all it takes for the phone to start ringing."[205]

Loftus's phone may have been ringing in January 1996 following her resignation from the American Psychological Association. The January issue of the *Washington State Bar News* announced they were "honored" to present excerpts from Dr. Elizabeth Loftus's speech upon receiving the Distinguished Contribution Award from the American Academy of Forensic Psychology: "Repressed Memory Litigation: Court Cases and Scientific Findings on Illusory Memory."

Repression is folklore, Loftus told her audience. Repressed memory litigation is not about child abuse in general, she assured them, nor is it about genuine victims who always remembered the abuse. Rather it's typified by cases in which memories appear impossible. Loftus failed to inform her audience that Washington State allowed civil suits to be filed based on *both* recovered and always-remembered memories of abuse.

Thirteen lawyers and two non-lawyers with expertise in trauma responded to the article, criticizing the *Bar News* for failing to report the trauma side of recovered memories. Attorney Barbara Jo Levy (see *Crook v. M.* in part 1) served as lead author. The letter cited recent research showing that a significant percentage of adults molested as children report forgetting some or all of the abuse. The letter writers suggested that an article for attorneys on memory should have addressed the whole picture. They noted, "Loftus herself was a victim to such a traumatic memory loss as she describes it on page 149 of her book, *Witness for the Defense.*"

Editor Hal White postponed publication of their response until the next month, describing it as "too long." White gave Loftus equal space to respond in the next issue. He deleted all the signators except for Barbara Jo Levy. Loftus criticized Levy's mention of Loftus's memory loss following her childhood molestation by a babysitter. She cited Fredrick Crews who condemned what he called "repressed memory therapy" as leading to "bizarre revelations."

In White's May 20 letter to the *Bar* leadership, he described Levy as "disgruntled," "frothing,' "wring[ing] her hands," and "having no knowledge but much supposition and vitriol." Her inferences, he said, "should be embarrassing" and are "incorrect and inflammatory toward me."

White left the *Bar News* in 1997 and published "The Mysteries of Reverend Dean."

The Washington State Bar Association Board of Governors named Steve Anderson—the attorney representing Seattle therapist David Calof—as the recipient of its 1998 Courageous Award in recognition of Anderson's perseverance under extreme personal attack by false memory advocates.

The Washington Post

The Post earned a solid reputation in the 1970s for its hard-hitting, double-sourced investigation of the Watergate scandal. Seattle therapist David Calof described his experience in 1994 with *Washington Post* reporter Sandra G. Boodman. "We talked for over an hour," Calof said. "I challenged false memory claims. I tried to make her see how research supported recovered memories. I was up until two in the morning faxing studies and articles showing childhood trauma could be repressed and corroborated."

Calof said he was surprised when he read Boodman's article. "At 28, Kathy O'Conner of Arlington says she remembered that her father raped her. She sued him and lost. Are delayed memories like hers true or false?" [206] He called Boodman to ask why she had not mentioned any of the research he sent.

"Your facts didn't fit the story we were doing," she replied.

"Like many of us back then," Calof says today, "I thought the media just needed some research corroborating traumatic amnesia. If they got the facts, they would report the facts. So I provided those facts. They weren't interested."

The facts Calof provided fit Boodman's 2002 story of a multiple-victim, priest abuse case. "How Deep the Scars of Abuse?" tells the story of two men who recovered memories of childhood sexual abuse by a priest.

Arizona Daily Star

Kristi Mattson, MD, learned of the Foundation's success in influencing academics when she attended a conference in 1998 that was required to maintain her medical license. Midway through a presentation titled "Recovered Memory: Clinical and Legal Issues," Mattson says she heard the presenter, a local psychiatry professor, name her family and state his belief that her family's experience was a case of false memories. Five local sisters, the speaker claimed, were all separately influenced by their therapists to have memories of abuse by their father.

"I'm the oldest of those five sisters," Mattson said in an interview. "I was shocked to hear this professor describing our family like that. He didn't contact me to fact-check the story. He just repeated what he read in the local newspaper."
In 1990, Mattson and her sisters recalled sexual abuse committed by their father, Roy Mattson, who would later chair an FMSF state chapter. The sisters independently sought therapy. The court granted Kristi Mattson a series of protective orders against her father, whom she had described as an alcoholic and a retired professor of electrical engineering at the University of Arizona.

The daughters settled their lawsuit in 1994.

In his ethics complaint against two of their therapists, Roy Mattson said he and his wife had dined with Pamela and Peter Freyd and Dr. Martin Orne in November 1991. The dinner, he reported, led to the founding of the FMS Foundation. Roy's complaints against the therapists were unanimously dismissed by the state board on October 14, 1994.

"I have a valid, state-sponsored investigative finding determining that no therapist gave me any 'false memories,'" Kristi says.

Following the board's dismissal, *Arizona Daily Star* reporter Joe Salkowski contacted Kristi and her sister for an interview. "Salkowski interrogated us much like our father's attorney had done," Kristi said. "He was angry and insistent. He asked us if we could have imagined the abuse, or dreamed it. We laughed out of nervousness. Salkowski told readers we giggled."

She provided Salkowski with a photo of her grinning father exposing himself. Salkowski failed to mention the shocking photo in his article. He knew about their father's complaint, she said, but he failed to mention that it was investigated and dismissed.

Kristi sent a letter to the *Star* pointing out the errors in Salkowski's three-part series. The *Star* did not respond.

"I still feel a bit wary around the neighbors and friends I knew in high school," she says. "For many of them, I'm probably still that daughter they read about who supposedly falsely accused her father."

Kristi Mattson is semiretired.

Roy Mattson died in 2013.

Joe Salkowski became the senior director of communications and public affairs at Tucson Electric Power.

The Sun

> "It's often said that a traumatic experience early in life marks a person forever, pulls her out of line, saying, 'Stay there. Don't move.'"

—Jeffrey Eugenides, *The Sun*, 2016

> "Strangers seem uncomfortable when you question them about their childhood. But really, what else are you going to talk about in line at the liquor store? Childhood trauma seems like the natural choice since it's the reason why most of us are in line there to begin with."

—Jenny Lawson, *Let's Pretend This Never Happened,* 2012, *The Sun*, 2016

The Sun describes itself as evoking "the splendor and heartache of being human." As a long-time subscriber, I was surprised to find that even this progressive magazine did not challenge the claims of an accused parent. A chapter from accused father Mark Pendergrast's *Victims of Memory*, "Daughters Lost," showed up in the June 1995 issue. Particularly troubling was senior editor Andrew Snee's introduction, so typical of the false memory rhetoric of the time: "Eventually, he [Mark Pendergrast] concluded that his family had been ripped apart, his children harmed by pseudoscientific therapy heavily slanted toward recovering memories of childhood sexual abuse and incest." Like other publications, *The Sun* failed to contact Pendergrast's daughters to fact-check the validity of their father's dramatic account.

Curious, I contacted Snee and asked why they published the chapter. They had received a copy of the book, he said, and since they were struggling to find articles back then, they decided to publish a chapter. "We haven't kept up with him or his foundation in the interim," Snee said.

Twenty years later, *The Sun* addressed traumatic amnesia in an interview with neuroscientist Dr. Bruce Perry. "The younger you are when the trauma occurs, the more likely you are to dissociate because a toddler who is sexually abused can't fight or flee . . . all she has left is to retreat into her inner world," Perry said.[207]

Three years later, nature writer Barry Lopez described the childhood rapes he experienced as a "devastating, disorienting experience." Lopez said that when he speaks to a group, he may see a man, see the body language, and he'll know. "It's unmistakable, the look in the face of a man who has been traumatized and then for years has felt isolated."[208]

Mansplaining the Mall Study

"Mansplaining" occurs when someone, typically a man, condescendingly explains something to another individual, typically a female, who knows more than he does about the subject. The popular press has been "mansplaining" the lost-in-a-mall study to us for thirty years. The following statements appeared in 2015 on the mall study's twentieth anniversary.

Tara Parker-Pope simplified the study for The *New York Times* in February. She omitted the interviews and said a quarter of the subjects believed they were lost after the first reading.

Douglas Starr in *The New Yorker* was generous in his claim that six subjects wove in sensory and emotional details.

Judge Alex Kozinski of the Ninth Circuit was also generous. He increased the published result of five (or six) to seven subjects in the *Georgetown Law Journal* in June. (Kozinski resigned in 2017 after fifteen women reported he allegedly made explicit remarks about them, exposed them to pornography, and touched them inappropriately.)

Susan Seligman in the summer issue of *Radcliffe Magazine* was brief. "Loftus can make people 'remember' that as children they were briefly lost in a mall" (pp. 10–11).

Huffington Post contributor Leigh Blickley reduced the subject count from twenty-four to four and reported, "Three out of the four respondents claimed to remember."[209]

Perhaps Richard Beck in his 2015 book, "We Believe the Children" comes closest to getting it right when he calls the mall study "a kind of shorthand" (p. 249). For many, the study has become shorthand for dismissing the sex abuse allegations of family members and friends as false memories.

Before his death in 2015, neurologist Oliver Sacks made implanting a memory seem easy in "Speak Memory" for *The New York Review of Books* in February 2013. He said Loftus simply suggested to a subject that he experienced a fictitious event.

The Other Side

As the media and psychology textbooks dismissed the child sex abuse allegations of adults, some academics raised concerns regarding the validity of the key study supporting false memory claims.

> 1997: *A getting-lost-in-a-mall memory is easier to implant than being molested as a child.* Psychologists Kathy Pezdek, Kimberly Finger, and Danelle Hodge used the subjects' older relatives to validate the stories. Three of the eighteen subjects said they got lost. None were convinced of an event similar to sexual assault—a childhood enema.[210]

> 2006: *Failed to control for cueing subjects.* Loftus and Pickrell failed to ensure the subjects weren't cued by interviewers to respond in a certain way. Loftus was deposed in *Paul Liano v. The Roman Catholic Church of the Diocese of Phoenix* in 2006.

> Q. But in that [mall] study did you control for demand characteristics [subjects are cued to respond in a certain way]?

A. I don't remember what we did to address the demand characteristics.

Q. Did you control for response bias [subjects respond based on what they think the researchers want to hear]?

A. I don't remember that we did that (p. 211).

2013: *The mall study may not be admissible in court.* Frye and Daubert standards determine if research is admissible in court. Law professor Wendy Murphy and her colleagues Megan Mitchell and Alexa Sardina noted the study's lack of a control group, its small sample size, and high error rate. Thus the mall study may not be admissible as scientific evidence depending on how Daubert and Frye are applied in a particular jurisdiction.[211]

2016: *Loftus says better studies have found similar results.* The "better" studies also tell subjects their relative witnessed the incident. Psychologists Bernice Andrews and Chris Brewin point out, "Although therapists may repeatedly suggest that events such as childhood abuse have happened, they are never in this position of being able to confirm events *because they themselves* [or their client's older relative] *were there.*"[212]

2019: *Reviewers found no evidence that any memories were implanted in the mall study.* As noted, Crook (this author) and McEwen (2019)[213] and Blizard and Shaw (2019)[214] analyzed the mall study and found no evidence that any of the mall study subjects were convinced they were lost. These findings suggest that the childhood sex abuse allegations should not be judged based on false memory claims.

Chapter 14

Navigating the Lost-in-a-Mall Study

"The Formation of False Memories,"[215] better known as the lost-in-a-mall study by Elizabeth Loftus, PhD, and Jacqueline Pickrell, has dominated our beliefs about sex abuse for nearly thirty years. We're told that since subjects were convinced they were lost in a mall, then adults can be convinced they were sexually assaulted as a child. The study has been cited over 1,700 times according to Google Scholar. Yet like a medical device that is funded for years and fails to live up to expectations, the mall study has been coasting along for three decades without any supporting evidence.

After seven months, Loftus convinced the Human Subjects Review Committee chair to approve the study on August 10, 1992. Twenty-four subjects would receive four stories, three true and one false, about their childhood. The false stories about getting lost included the following true details:

- where the family shopped when the subject was about five years old,

- which family members were present,

- what might have attracted the subject, and

- verification by the relative that the subject was not lost at a mall at age five (approximately thirteen years earlier).

The false stories implied the subject's older relative was present when the subject supposedly became lost. The subjects wrote about the four stories. They were interviewed twice (or three times according to some accounts), then asked to identify the false story.

"Memory works a little bit more like a Wikipedia page," Loftus told her TED Talk audience in 2013. "You can go in there and change it, but so can other people."[216] Researchers, it seems, can also go in and change their results. The following timeline is a detailed account of what occurred "backstage" at the University of Washington during the mall study's circuitous, four-year-long journey to publication.

1991: "Implanted by Therapists" Selected

"Implanted memories" was selected as the basis for dismissing adults' child sex abuse allegations following *The Washington Post* headline, "Delayed Lawsuits of Sexual Abuse on the Rise; Alleged Victims Base Legal Actions on Memories Critics Say May Be Implanted in Therapy," on August 14, 1991.

1991: "Lost" Memories Implanted in Younger Relatives

Loftus asked her students to implant a memory of getting lost in someone. James Coan convinced his younger brother he was lost but failed to convince his mother that her younger son was lost. Lost memories were implanted in four additional subjects by older relatives who implied they were present at the time. Coan was assigned to head the official lost-in-a-mall study in January 1992. He began a seven-month-long journey to obtain approval for the study from the Human Subjects Review Committee at the University of Washington.

July 1992: "Implanted" Defense Introduced to the Public

Dan Goleman with *The New York Times* interviewed Loftus and introduced her "implanted memories" theory to the public. He described Coan's success with his younger brother as "pertinent."

1993: First Six Subjects Correctly Identify the False Story

Following the study's approval, Coan failed to implant any

false memories in the first six subjects (Coan's senior paper, "Creating False Memories," pp. 16–17, August 18, 1993). Jacqueline Pickrell, another undergraduate, was appointed to head the study.

1994: Loftus Testifies the First Six Subjects Were Dropped

Q: In your discussion of being able to implant memories in people, are you using those first six subjects?

A: No, not the first six. (Loftus deposition in *Crook v. M.*, p. 60, 1/24/94).

1994: Memories of Getting Lost Implanted: None

Twenty-four subjects were each given four stories, three were true. If the lost story was credible, then each story would have an equal chance of being chosen as false—and six subjects would believe they were lost. The final report to the University of Washington Human Subjects Review Committee on June 1, 1994, states memories were implanted in two subjects. *24 subjects have been run. About 8–9% [two participants] have formed false memories. Another 10–15% formed partial false memories* [remembered parts of the story and speculated how it might have happened, p. 722]. The memories appear to be less clear and vivid than true memories.

Two subjects are described in the published study. (1) The Hillsdale subject used logic to determine the lost story was false (p. 723), leaving the K-Mart subject. (2) The K-Mart subject's response appears in a chapter titled "The Reality of Illusory Memories"[217] in a book titled Memory Distortions: How Minds, Brains, and Societies Reconstruct the Past. There, it's evident the subject did get lost and corrected her relative's story. "I vaguely remember walking around K-Mart crying and looking for Tien and Tuan. I thought I was lost forever. I went to the shoe department because we always spent a lot of time there. I went to the handkerchief place because we were there last. I circled all over the store it seemed 10 times. I just remember walking around crying. I do not remember the Chinese woman or the ICEE (but it would be raspberry ICEE if I was getting an ICEE) part. I don't even remember being found" (p. 63).

No false memories were implanted in the mall study. However, the false memory story for abuse accusations had gone viral by the time the two-subject result was reported to the HSRC in June 1994. Loftus responded by inflating the mall study result for publication.

1995: Published Result: Five/Six Subjects

The mall study result was inflated from zero to five or six subjects (both appear on p. 723) and published as "The Formation of False Memories" in the December 1995 issue of *Psychiatric Annals*.

2019: Two Reviews Report Mall Study Result as Zero

Two detailed reviews of the study in 2019 found the twenty-four subjects all correctly identified the false story.[218, 219] No false memories were implanted in the mall study.

Inflated Data in Academia and the Legal Arena

Some have wondered why *Psychiatric Annals* accepted the mall study for publication. Marta Sierra-Garcia and Uri Gneezy (2021) suggest that when a paper is more interesting, reviewers may lower their standards.[220] As noted, the false memory story had gone viral by the time the study was published in December 1995.

"Academics who cut corners for personal gain can count themselves in the majority," a 2022 survey of Dutch researchers found.[221] Loftus cites the inflated mall study result while testifying as an expert and billing up to $600 per hour.

Social psychologist Anthony Greenwald suggests, "A report of potential conflict of interest associated with expert witness service could routinely be requested of authors in submitting testimony-relevant articles" (p. 34).[222] There is no evidence that a statement of potential conflict of interest was requested by *Psychiatric Annals* for "The Formation of False Memories." The guest editor for the special issue titled, "Recovered Memories: True and False" was Susan L. McElroy, MD, a specialist in pharmacology.

The mall study is not the only testimony-relevant, unsupported research Loftus has published. Mary Koss, Shannon Tromp, and Melinda Tharan reported that the abstract for Loftus and Burns[223] is not supported by the data reported on page 320 of the article.[224] Special counsel Patrick Fitzerald pointed out another misrepresentation during his cross-examination of Loftus in the *Libby* hearing.[225] The abstract for "Beyond the Ken" [226] is not supported by the data reported in the appendix of the article.

Loftus explains, "Each individual can decide what strategy best suits him or her, and let the survival of the fittest expert prevail. Those who misrepresent facts of studies will eventually be discovered. Admittedly it may take the system some time to discover who these people are. But after this discovery they will no longer be welcome in court."[227]

"Academic fraud is not only a crime, it is a threat to the intellectual integrity upon which the evolution of knowledge rests," says Rene Cantu with the University of Houston Division of Research.[228] "It also compromises the integrity of the institution, as any institution will take a blow to their reputation for allowing academic misconduct to go unnoticed under its watch."

The Mall Study at the University of Washington

The mall study was conducted from 1991 through 1995 at the University of Washington (UW) using university resources. Research misconduct at the UW is defined as (1) fabrication (making up data or results and recording or reporting them), (2) falsification (changing or omitting data so that the research is not accurately represented), and (3) plagiarism (appropriating another's ideas).[229] As defined by the UW, the mall study results were fabricated (made up) and falsified (not accurately represented).

Crook and McEwen (2019)[230] and Blizard and Shaw (2019)[231] documented how Loftus and Pickrell failed to implant any memories of getting lost in the study, then misrepresented the results for publication. If UW were informed of the misrepresentation, would they acknowledge the fabricated result and discontinue their support of the study? We decided to find out. In the interest of full disclosure, I informed the UW of my double alum status.

The two reviews together with letters summarizing the misreported findings were sent to UW officials with a request to discontinue support of the mall study. Ruth Blizard, PhD, described the consequences of the mall study in her letter, "For 25 years, survivors of childhood sexual abuse have suffered the legal and social consequences of Loftus's unwarranted interpretations of her research."

Julie Severson, PhD, director of the Office of Research Misconduct Proceedings at the UW, responded to our request on November 4, 2020. The allegations of misconduct were not sufficiently specific, she said, and it could not be determined that the study "is having or could have a substantial adverse effect on the health or safety of the public."

The UW stands by the fabricated mall study results.

Loftus transferred to UC Irvine in 2002. The UW maintains a staff website for Loftus. It is here that the UW fails to support the mall study. The study is not cited under "Articles."[232]

A New Approach

A new generation of researchers is taking a straightforward approach to examining memory accuracy. Diamond, Armson, and Levine in 2020 measured the memory accuracy of children and adults who participated in recent or long-ago verifiable events: a mask fitting and an audio-guided art tour of a hospital. Their memory accuracy rates were high, at 93 to 95 percent. Academics, perhaps influenced by the claims of false memory researchers, estimated the subjects' accuracy rates at 40 percent.[233]

Chapter 15

Going After Therapists

By 1994, the Foundation's media campaign had convinced the public that the child sex abuse accusations of adults are false memories. Survivors were silenced by relatives and acquaintances who insisted, "I read about false memories like yours," "Your parents must be devastated," "You saw a therapist, right?"

"It is now time to solve the crisis," Executive Director Pamela Freyd announced on the Foundation's second anniversary in a March 1994 newsletter. The Foundation turned its attention to a new project, suing therapists.

The Ramona lawsuit set the stage. Holly Ramona was a college student in 1990 when she recalled abuse by her father, Gary Ramona, vice-president of marketing for Robert Mondavi Winery. Her father filed a third-party lawsuit against her therapists in 1991 claiming $8M in damages. Named as defendants were therapist Marche Isabella, psychiatrist Richard Rose, and the Western Medical Center of Anaheim.

Gary Ramona stood in the hallway during breaks in the 1994 trial, pitching his falsely accused story to reporters from the *Napa Valley Register*, *The New York Times*, *Hard Copy*, and the London's *Daily Mail*. The jury awarded $475,000 to Ramona, considerably less than his substantial $1M in legal expenses.[234] The Foundation newsletter cited twenty-six supportive articles (June 1994).

Following the decision, Jury foreman Thomas Dudum told Katy

Butler with the *Los Angeles Times*, "I want to make it clear that we did not believe, as Gary indicates, that these therapists gave Holly a wonder drug and implanted those memories. It was an uneasy decision, and there were lots of unanswered questions."[235]

Shawna, Holly's sister, challenged Moira Johnston Block's false memory version of their case.

"Sister Challenges 'Evidence' Book's Facts," *San Francisco Chronicle*, August 3, 1997, p. 4.

> As the sister of Holly Ramona, I feel compelled to write you and dispel any notion that Moira Johnston Block's new book, "Spectral Evidence," contains any facts. I have heard this woman promote her fictional account of my family's tragedy and cannot imagine that the public would believe her statements.
>
> In order to set the record straight, let me be clear that Ms. Block's implication of any reconciliation between my father and me is grossly inaccurate. In fact, there is no chance that my father and I will ever have a relationship with each other. My mother has been ill and will always be my only parent. She is the only parent who has ever loved and protected me.
>
> The courage that my sister, Holly, and my mother have demonstrated in these difficult times is an inspiration to me. They have shown me the utmost integrity. I believe that both Moira Johnston Block and Gary Ramona are disconnected from our world of truth and justice. It would be unfortunate for others to believe their view of the world.
>
> My family (Holly, Kelli, Mom and I) has had to overcome the past seven years with dignity and strength. Unfortunately, even after all of this time, society is still enthralled by our pain. But this is made worse by Ms. Block's book, which only perpetuates the falsehoods.
>
> Shawna Ramona
> *St. Helena, CA*[236]

Block responded:

Sunday, August 3rd's *San Francisco Chronicle* vividly bared the venomous anger, the loggerhead disagreements, and the human pain that continue to spew from the recovered memory wars. The Book Review published a letter from Gary Ramona's youngest daughter, Shawna, an attack on my book about the landmark Ramona case, *Spectral Evidence*, and on the media in general for continuing to be "enthralled by our pain."

Holly dropped her lawsuit against her father and went on to earn a graduate degree in psychology.

Gary Ramona is vice-president of marketing for Antigal Winery and Estates.

Like Shooting Fish in a Barrel

Attorneys gathered at the Westin Hotel in Seattle in 1994 for a workshop on filing civil suits against therapists. Clinical social worker and psychotherapist Joan Golston covered the story for *Treating Abuse Today*.[237]

Dallas attorney Skip Simpson made it seem easy and profitable. He assured his audience, "It doesn't matter what kind of law you practice . . . you can win in every case . . . I'm telling you, a blow-up doll can handle these cases . . . It's like shooting fish in a barrel. We sue, and the juries [insurance companies] are eager to fill that dump truck with money . . . In retractor cases, it's usually going to be a six-figure plus settlement."[238] He explained, "We have the studs on our side, the McHughs, and the Loftuses."

Simpson and his colleagues represented retractors, former patients who sued therapists for malpractice, claiming their memories were implanted. Retractors' dramatic accounts of what they had remembered were not challenged by the press. Insurance carriers settled the lawsuits rather than take them to trial.[239] The plaintiffs' attorneys received a third of the settlement. Their experts billed hundreds of dollars per hour to review the case. Plaintiffs' received the remainder, minus other expenses. A Microsoft Word search revealed that lawsuit mentions in the Foundation's monthly newsletters rose to fifty-four in 1994, to eighty-one in 1995, and peaked at eighty-seven in 1997.

Memories and Millionaires: The False Litigant Syndrome

The following segment is based on "Inadequate Legal Representation of Therapists Accused of Implanting False Memories: Three Case Studies" which I presented in 2002 at the 19th annual conference of the International Society for the Study of Dissociation in Baltimore.[240] *To prepare for this presentation, I conducted in-depth examinations of the testimony of three high-profile retractors who sued their therapists.*

Law professor Alan Scheflin and psychologist Dan Brown reviewed the medical records of thirty former patients who sued their therapists. The plaintiffs were all in contact with false memory influences before suing the former therapists.

Their review found that the female clients were severely ill before seeking therapy.[241] Their memories were not suggested by the therapist; instead, they were reported by the client, or as in the Burgus case, by other patients. Clinically significant, factitious, attention-seeking behaviors were a factor with 33 percent of the plaintiffs. In 43 percent of the cases, the plaintiffs displayed symptoms of dissociative disorders long before they met the defendants. Medical records showed the patients' treatment was within the standard of care, and they improved during treatment.

The media highlighted three retractors—Laura Pasley in Dallas, Mary Shanley in Houston and Pat Burgus in Chicago. The women were represented by Skip Simpson of Texas, Zachary Bravos of Illinois, and Chris Barden of Minnesota.

Laura Pasley: Accused Parents in Search of a Lawsuit

Before seeing a therapist, Laura Pasley left Dallas Baptist College during her first semester and found a clerical job with the police department. She dated police officers. She overdosed after the first two relationships ended. She began seeing a married officer and gave birth to their daughter in 1980 (deposition, p. 316, 326).[242] She informed the Dallas chief of police in a letter dated November 15, 1984, that she had filed a paternity suit against the father of her daughter.

Pasley entered treatment with Michael Moore in Dallas after suffering from bulimia for twenty-two years. Her mental health improved. Her compulsive spending became less of a problem (deposition, p. 347). She turned her whip, handcuffs, and knife over to Moore for safekeeping (p. 230). She called Moore once or more each day (deposition, p. 174). Previously a loner, she began to develop friendships. Her anger problems lessened. Midway through her therapy with Moore, Pasley self-published *Hungry Heart Line*, a newsletter for fellow bulimics. She created a new life for herself in the November 1987 issue.

> It is hard to believe that an only child from a nice middle-class family who appears so happy on the outside was actually crying out for help on the inside . . . I married my high school "sweetheart" my junior year in college. He was a perfectionist and a very disciplined individual. He had to be. Professional athletes are trained to be scheduled and structured . . . We had big homes and nice cars but there was still such emptiness inside of me.

Pasley was behind in her therapy payments when Moore asked her to sign a release so that insurance payments would go directly to him. Instead, she stopped seeing Moore. She read Glenna Whitley's "The Seduction of Gloria Grady" in *D Magazine*.[243] Pasley had known Gloria Grady during her treatment with Moore. She contacted Gloria's parents, who invited her to join them at the home of an accused father. The father told Pasley, "You really need to go and see a lawyer about this [your case]" (deposition, pp. 398–402). The parents accompanied Pasley to her first appointment with Dallas attorney Skip Simpson.

Pasley and her daughter sued Moore, group co-facilitator Lee Flournoy, and the Richardson Medical Center. In her deposition, Pasley described abuse by her mother (deposition, p. 144), her father, and her older brother (p. 148).

She interviewed with *Primetime Live* as her attorney completed the settlement negotiations for a reportedly moderate amount.

Pasley described the Foundation members: "I cherish these people and all they have done to enhance my life." As for those who did not retract their accusations, Laura said she wanted to "wring their necks."[244]

Michael Moore found employment in another field.

Laura Pasley lives in Texas.

Mary Shanley: More Stories

Shanley told *Frontline's* "Search for Satan" viewers in 1995 that she got worse during therapy. When she stopped therapy, she got better.[245]

After her lawsuit against her Spring Shadows Glen therapists settled, Shanley traveled to Houston to testify in the criminal trial against her former therapist, Judith Peterson, PhD, and others. Under cross-examination by Peterson's trial attorney, Rusty Hardin, Shanley conceded that before she saw her first therapist, she experienced blackouts following a hysterectomy. She disappeared during those blackouts. When found, she was incoherent and unable to recognize her family members. She experienced panic attacks, self-harming episodes, and angry outbursts. After three hospitalizations for dissociative episodes, Shanley entered Spring Shadows Glen in Houston where her treatment was supervised by Peterson. Her mental health improved, and she was eventually able to live on her own. Shanley conceded that her therapy at Spring Shadows had helped her become stronger, more assertive, and a better communicator. After the government had presented its case for five months, the charges against the Spring Shadows Glen defendants were dismissed (also see chapter 7).

Pat Burgus: Hurting So Bad

Pat Burgus was threatening to kill herself and others in 1982 when she sought help from social worker Anne-Marie Baughman. In an interview with the *Des Moines Reporter* Baughman described what she observed: "The muscles in her face would all relax . . . and she would just look different. It was just the eeriest thing." Baughman referred Burgus to Rush-Presbyterian in Chicago for further treatment.

The statute of limitations for filing a malpractice lawsuit had run out for Burgus by 1993. "Patty sounded very troubled when she called me," Bennett Braun, MD, her former psychiatrist, said in an interview. "She said she was hurting so bad. I believed her, and I felt sorry for her. So I agreed to see her, knowing this would reinstate the statute of limitations and she might sue me." Burgus and her sons sued Braun and others in 1994.

Braun added, "We had to get a protection order in the mid-1990s to stop attorneys from recruiting patients to sue us. They were contacting the patients using the pay phone on the 10-patient unit." He continued, "Back in the 1980s, we were doing the best we could with some very troubled patients referred to our facility."[246] Nine patients eventually sued Braun and others. Braun's insurance carrier replaced the original defense attorney, Deborah Davy, who had won twenty-three out of twenty-five malpractice cases, with another attorney with no trial experience and who had handled only a few $20,000 cases.

Pat Burgus and her two sons named Braun, Rush Presbyterian St. Luke's Medical Center, and Elva Poznanski—the Burgus sons' psychiatrist. *Frontline* featured Burgus and Shanley in their 1995 documentary, "Search for Satan."

Deposed on December 2, 1996, Pat Burgus testified that she told the hospital staff, "I'm switching (personalities) out of control today. I'm doing so much switching today I can't believe it." The rapid switching decreased over time as her psychiatrist increased her medication dosages.

Deposed on January 17, 1997, Burgus testified her psychiatrist did not implant any memories. The attorney asked Burgus about the source of her memories. She named two—herself and other patients on the ward. Braun had not implanted any memories.

> **Ringel:** *Any detail or scenario, anything that mentioned you having been the victim of abuse, did any of it come from any place other than being initially uttered through your mouth?*
>
> **Pat:** *Yes.*

Ringel: *What?*

Pat: *He would often come to me with information from other patients (p. 913).*

The Settlement

As the *Burgus* trial was set to begin, the three insurance carriers settled with Burgus and her two sons for the largest amount to date, $10.6M on October 31, 1997. The defendants admitted to no wrongdoing. Pat Burgus's share of the settlement was $3M—minus her attorney's $1M fee and her share of the fees for the six experts, including William Grove, PhD; James Hudson, MD; Elizabeth Loftus, PhD; Paul McHugh, MD; Richard Ofshe, PhD; and August Piper, MD. Each expert billed hundreds of dollars per hour to review the plaintiffs' depositions and case records. The Burgus sons, John and Mikey, shared the remaining $7.6M, minus their share of the experts' fees and their attorneys' $1.52M fee.[247] The attorney assigned to Braun's defense billed the insurance carrier $1.3M.

News of the $10.6M settlement attracted attention within legal circles. In another lawsuit (the source asked to remain anonymous), the defense attorney's opening remarks on the plaintiff's "money-grab" had jurors smiling. The plaintiff's attorney made a settlement offer after lunch. The defense countered with a much lower offer. The offer was accepted.

While FMSF efforts generated lawsuits, recruitment ads by law firms were less successful. Goldberg & Osborne in Phoenix ran, "Have you been diagnosed with DID?" The ad failed to generate any clients.[248] A similar ad by Stanley, Mandel & Iola in the *Dallas Morning News* generated one client.

"That case should have gone to trial," Braun says today. "My AIG policy gave me the right to make that decision. I paid a premium to ensure this. But they insisted on settling. We would have shown that we didn't implant any false memories. Who knows? If this lawsuit had gone to trial back then, maybe treatment for traumatized patients would be further along than it is today."

Both the insurance companies and clinicians might have benefitted if the lawsuit had gone forward. Since Burgus conceded in her deposition that Braun did not implant any memories, her testimony may have resulted in a favorable decision for the defendants. Since the raw data for the mall study were subpoenaed by the defense, the media might have discovered that the mall study subjects all correctly identified the "lost" story as false.

Following the settlement, Burgus filed an ethics complaint against Braun.[249] Statement #30 in the complaint claims, "At the time of her admission to the Rush psychiatric unit, Patti did not suffer from mental illness which required in-patient treatment." Braun says, "I had so many people on my waiting list that if she didn't need admission I would have just taken the next one down."[250] Braun's license was suspended for two years, and he was placed on probation for five years.[251]

Burgus agreed to an interview with *Chicago Magazine* writer Cynthia Hanson in 1998 on the condition that Hanson would not have access to the information in her deposition or hospital records. Hanson agreed to her terms.[252]

Patricia Burgus lives in Iowa.

Braun moved to Montana where he regained his license to practice. He was named in a lawsuit in May 2019.[253] The case settled for a modest amount.

Braun retired and cares for his wife who was diagnosed with terminal cancer.

Chapter 16

Memory Wars: The Dark Side

_____

The Memory Wars, as portrayed by the media, are an academic debate. Are memories of childhood trauma easily implanted by therapists? Was hypnosis involved? Were books involved? Were the memories triggered by sexual fantasies? Were they an easy solution for other problems?

Pulitzer Prize-winning reporter Mike Stanton investigated the Foundation and concluded, "The Foundation is an aggressive, well-financed PR machine adept at manipulating the press, harassing its critics, and mobilizing a diverse army of psychiatrists, outspoken academics, expert defense witnesses, litigious lawyers, Freud bashers, critics of psychotherapy, and devastated parents," in his article for the *Columbia Journalism Review*.[254]

"Silencing the victim/witness and concealment of the crime is a horrifyingly reasonable motive for abusers of children," Seattle psychologist Laura Brown writes.[255] Brown describes the parallels between child molesters aggressively silencing their victims and false memory supporters doing the same with their critics.

Psychologist Anna Salter called the Wars, "A political fight between a group of well-financed people whose freedom, livelihood, finances, reputation, or liberty are being threatened by disclosures of child sexual abuse and—on the other hand—a group of well-meaning, ill-organized, underfinanced, and often terribly naïve academics who expect fair play."[256]

Silencing the Accusations

The accounts below describe the Foundation's response to those who challenged false memory claims. Other articles may have been retracted or canceled due to similar efforts. False memory articles have mysteriously appeared on the beds of hospitalized clients. Some survivors, myself included, have received anonymous letters supporting lawsuits against therapists. Others have received anonymous mailings with a crude drawing depicting caricatures of named therapists atop a waste-disposal site.

Institute of Pennsylvania Hospital Notebook

A 1992 story in the Institute of Pennsylvania Hospital newsletter resulted in one of the earliest efforts by false memory advocates to censor media coverage. The article began . . . "Sheila felt like she had been victimized twice. First by the father who raped her at age 10 when her mother was away, and then by the therapist who asked if she could be making the story up. 'Many little girls fantasize about sleeping with their daddies,' Sheila was told after finally gathering the courage to see a therapist 20 years later."

"A skilled psychotherapist will attempt to detect and help a patient sort out memory distortions in the course of treatment," explained Richard Kluft, MD, director of the institute's dissociative disorders program.[257]

Foundation Executive Director Pamela Freyd and her husband, Peter, contacted the hospital and demanded the article be retracted. They claimed the article was inaccurate.[258]

"I agreed to meet with Pamela and Peter Freyd in my office," Kluft said in an interview. The Freyds warned me that Roseanne Barr's and LaToya Jackson's families would sue me if the article were not retracted." He added, "I understood the Freyds to be conveying a threat rather than attempting to enter a dialogue." No lawsuits were filed.

Psychology of Women Newsletter

University of Rhode Island psychology professor Kat Quina's editorial in the *Psychology of Women Newsletter* in 1994 received a similar response. Quina discussed issues that were not widely reported by the press: Jennifer Freyd's description of the Freyd family dynamics, Ralph Underwager's resignation from the board following a pro-pedophilia statement, and psychologist Elizabeth Loftus's promotion of malpractice actions against therapists in the American Bar Association's *ABA Journal* in 1993.

Pamela Freyd described the editorial as a "personal attack based on hearsay." Underwager and Wakefield described Quina's statements as "false and defamatory" and said they had sent the editorial to their attorney.

The editorial was not retracted; there were no lawsuits.[259]

Law & Social Inquiry

Lynne Henderson, a law professor at Indiana University, reviewed books by Jennifer L. Freyd, Daniel L. Schacter, Elizabeth Loftus and Katherine Ketcham, and Richard Ofshe and Ethan Watters for the American Bar Foundation's *Law & Social Inquiry*.[260]

Pam Freyd asked for evidence regarding several statements, including Henderson's description of Jennifer Freyd as an abuse victim. Pam sent letters to the president and the executive director of the American Bar Association in April 1998. She claimed the journal had "published false information and defamatory comments with impunity." She warned, "Last month, one person resigned and two people were fired at CNN because they reported a false story . . . I expect that in the absence of evidence, you will provide a full and printed retraction of these statements."

The CNN story involved Pulitzer Prize–winning journalist Peter Arnett who was reprimanded for his work on the story of the United States military using lethal sarin nerve gas during a secret 1970 mission in Laos. News producers April Oliver and Jack Smith refused to resign and were dismissed. Senior executive producer Pamela Hill resigned.

The journal editors reviewed Henderson's article. They did not retract the article.

The Toronto Star

"The Foundation's promotion of a defense for a crime they were accused of was patently self-serving,"[261] *Toronto Star* columnist

Michelle Landsberg pointed out in 1993. She said she was skeptical of accused parents who approached her with their tragic stories. She had attended a Criminal Lawyers Association conference, she said, where "one speaker, James Alcock of York University, compared incest survivors to people who say they were abducted by UFOs."

The *Star* received dozens of letters from parents complaining about the Landsberg article. Pamela and Peter Freyd filed a complaint with the Ontario Press Council alleging that Landsberg's column was false in various respects. The complaint was dropped.

The Parliamentary Library Report

Patricia Begin, a researcher in the Parliamentary Library in Toronto, wrote a background paper for parliament members on memories of childhood sexual abuse. The conflict between the accuser and the accused, she said, "comes down to a comparison of their memories and personal credibility . . . false allegations are rare, not all memories recovered in a therapeutic setting are false."

Toronto Star legal affairs reporter Tracey Tyler wrote that some of Canada's "leading medical and legal experts" say that the Begin background paper is "dangerously biased." Tyler named the experts— Alan Gold, an attorney who represented defendants accused of sex abuse; Foundation board member Dr. Harold Merskey; and executive director Pamela Freyd.

The *Star*'s ombudsman dismissed the claims, concluding that Tyler's story "lacked context and balance" and "distorted Begin's conclusions."[262]

The Witch-Hunt Narrative

Author Ross Cheit, PhD, reports that days before the publication of the hardcover edition of his book, writer Debbie Nathan contacted his publisher with a libel threat. She said she knew she had been libeled in Cheit's *The Witch-Hunt Narrative*. She would pursue legal remedies in the US and England if the book were published. She did not identify any offending passages. Cheit's book documents several errors and omissions in Nathan's writings. His book was published on schedule. Nathan did not file a lawsuit.[263] Cheit quotes Nathan who said that the sex abuse cases were impossible to believe in part because the alleged perpetrators were white and middle class (p. 180).[264]

Katy Butler: Censored

Reviewers portrayed *Making Monsters: False Memories, Psychotherapy, and Sexual Hysteria* by Richard Ofshe and Ethan Watters as an indictment of the therapy profession.[265] Journalist Katy Butler took an investigative approach in her review of the book in her article "Did Daddy Really Do It?" for the *Los Angeles Times* (see Chapter 6).[266] Ofshe responded to Butler's review in a February 26 letter, saying, "Simple incompetence does not explain this bizarre review."

Newsweek hired Butler to examine the media's uncritical acceptance of false memory claims and to report documented recovered memory cases. The magazine withdrew the offer, journalist Mike Stanton reported in "U-Turn on Memory Lane," following criticism of Butler by Foundation co-founders Pam and Peter Freyd and board members Richard Ofshe and Fredrick Crews.

Newsweek senior editor John Capoya told Stanton, "We weren't too sanguine about getting into a huge pissing match with these people." Similar articles may have been canceled due to complaints from false memory advocates.

Speaking at the national conference of Investigative Reporters and Editors in 1996, Butler said, "I've worked very hard to tell both sides of this story. What's interesting to me about all this is that telling both sides has started to seem like a dangerous and risky act."

Joe Williams: "Capturing the Friedmans"

Film critic Joe Williams reviewed "Capturing the Friedmans," a 2003 documentary featuring Arnold Friedman and his son, Jesse, for the *St. Louis Post Dispatch*. The two pled guilty to molesting children who attended after-school computer classes in the Friedman home. The Friedmans received prison sentences Arnold died. Many who viewed the film were left wondering about Jesse's guilt. Williams suggested the fuzzy perception of the Friedmans' guilt may have been the result of editing.

I emailed Williams, pointing out that the statements by a young man partially obscured by a shadow did not reflect his body language.

Williams forwarded the emails he'd received from authors Mark Pendergrast, Debbie Nathan, and Donald S. Connery; attorney Karyse Philip; professor Stephen Philion; reporters Katha Pollitt and Mark Sauer; educator Hannah MacLaren; physician Michael Kennedy; psychologist David Lotto; and Foundation member Michael Short.[267] The emails attacked Williams, describing him as a liar and a goofball. He was accused of "sick artistic license" and told he owed an apology to the Friedman son.

Sharon Simone: A False Memory Obituary

Harvard graduate Sharon Simone appeared on *20/20*, *Good Morning America*, and CBS's *Town Hall* after a jury in 1990 awarded $2.3M to Sharon and her sister Susan Hammond in their lawsuit against their father, former FBI agent Edward Roberts.

Marlo Thomas portrayed Simone in the CBS television movie, "Ultimate Betrayal." Together with Congresswoman Pat Schroeder, Simone helped pass The Child Abuse Accountability Act in 1994, allowing garnishment of federal pensions to satisfy judgments for child abuse. Simone described the 1996 reconciliation with her father. "Dad owned up . . . He said he was proud that I got that legislation passed. He understands why I did it. I said I was proud of him for getting sober and making room for a relationship with my family and me that was based upon truth and compassion."[268]

Recovered memories did not play a role in the trial—Simone and her sister had always remembered the abuse. When Simone returned to Colorado Springs for her father's funeral, she found the community had created a new version—the accusations were based on recovered memories. Andy Friedberg's obituary for the *Colorado Springs Gazette* announced, "'Repressed memory' figure, FBI investigator dies at 81. In recent years, some psychiatrists and mental health professionals have challenged the concept of repressed memories. Critics say that in some cases traumatic memories appear to stem from suggestions by therapists."

Her father's former boss, ex-district attorney Bob Russell, asked to speak first at the memorial service. Simone says Russell's eulogy quickly evolved into an angry defense of the deceased—a deny, attack, and reverse victim and offender (DARVO) approach. Directing his closing words to Simone and her sisters, Russell said, "And to you Rodgers children, let me say," his voice rising to a shout, "your father was an HONORABLE man." Russell left the podium and strode down the aisle and out the door of the chapel. The attendees, including forty law enforcement officers at the front of the chapel, sat in shocked silence.

Simone stepped up to the podium. She looked out over a sea of stunned faces and began, "It will be no surprise to the many gathered here that the Rodgers family has been in a process of healing in terms of our relationships with each other, and we are coming along in this regard, thankfully." She glanced down at her notes and began to speak.

Today Simone writes and speaks about healing the abuses of power, conscious and unconscious, that are threatening the Earth; thousands of species; and the survival of the generations to come who will be left with a polluted, ravaged biosphere. Simone says that her journey out of child abuse has given her insight into our capacity and proclivity to not look, to not see, our self-focused attitudes toward peoples, creatures, and the mountains and rivers she loves (email, 7/19/18).

"Lisa"

Dutch investigative journalist Sanne Terlingen covered the story of "Lisa," fifteen, who told authorities she was abused by her father and several other men working at the Ministry of Justice. When she gave birth, one of the men raped and killed her baby, she said, and buried the baby's body in the nearby woods. The prosecutor dropped the case and blamed the mother for "implanting" the memories after her divorce from the girl's father.

Child porn was found on Lisa's father's computer. A medical exam revealed Lisa had given birth. Search dogs found a child's body buried where Lisa said her baby was buried. The police refused to dig the site, still saying they found her story unbelievable. Terlingen said she was approached by a therapist who said her organization had treated forty people with similar stories. Nearly 150 people eventually reported similar experiences to Terlingen.

Terlingen received emails claiming the accusations were implanted memories. Terlingen says that most of the emails were from individuals associated with the Dutch chapter of the False Memory Syndrome Foundation.[269] Emails were sent to Terlingen's editor, claiming her investigation was a threat to public health. The text of Terlingen's 2020 documentary is online.[270]

The following accounts are a sampling of the lawsuits filed against therapists by false memory advocates.

Joyanna Silberg: A Leadership Role

Child psychologist Joyanna Silberg was one of many treatment providers who faced ethics complaints filed by parents accused of child abuse. Silberg retired as the coordinator of Trauma Disorders Services for Children at Sheppard Pratt Hospital in Baltimore. She has taken a leadership role in protecting children and confronting false memory claims. Silberg was the subject of ten board complaints, filed primarily by accused fathers, based on false memory allegations. The complaints were investigated and dismissed. Her legal fees amounted to nearly $150,000. She continues to face harassment as she testifies for children and protective parents in custody cases.

Ellen Lacter: Mandated Reporting

Psychologist Ellen Lacter was contacted by a mother in 2008 looking for resources and referrals for her son. Lacter did not treat, evaluate, or meet the woman or her son. In the course of their correspondence, the woman provided information suggesting that her son was abused, which required Lacter, as a mandated reporter, to file two reports of suspected child abuse. The mother killed her son in 2010 and was convicted of manslaughter.

Lucien Greaves (alias: Doug Mesner; birth name: Doug Misicko), founder of the Temple of Satan, submitted an Internet petition in 2016. The complaint asked the California Board of Psychology to revoke Lacter's license, falsely claiming she had contributed to the mother's murder of her son.

The California Board of Psychology found it unnecessary to interview Lacter before determining that she did not violate any laws or regulations.[271]

Charles Whitfield: Taking It to Court

Psychiatrist Charles Whitfield described the one-day, Foundation-sponsored seminar he attended. "The focus was mostly on how to silence or punish the assumed 'bad' outside influences that gave their accusing adult children their 'false' memories" (p. xvi).

Following the release of Whitfield's *Memory and Abuse*, an investigative approach to false memory claims, Pamela and Peter Freyd filed a lawsuit alleging that Whitfield acted with malice toward them by stating publicly during professional workshops that Peter Freyd had sexually abused his daughter and that Pamela had failed to protect her and was a co-abuser. The Freyds were represented by attorney Thomas Pavlinic.

US judge Benson Legg granted summary judgment to Whitfield in 1997. The Freyds filed a complaint with Whitfield's medical licensing board. The board dismissed their complaint.

Whitfield authored ten books and was named to Best Doctors in America. He died in December 2019.

Chapter 17

The False Memory Sieges

As researchers continued to corroborate recovered memories of childhood trauma,[272] many of those who challenged false memory claims were harassed for years by false memory supporters. These sieges drained the resources of the targeted individuals and impacted their families, their clients, and others.

Anna Salter, PhD: 1988 to 1993

For psychologist Anna Salter, it began in 1988 when she received a grant from the New England Association of Child Welfare Commissioners and Directors. The grant allowed Salter to examine claims that standard interviewing techniques for children resulted in false accusations. Salter focused on the work of Ralph Underwager and Hollida Wakefield, prominent spokespeople for false accusation claims. Salter reviewed their *Accusations of Child Sexual Abuse* and compared what they said about studies to what the studies reported.[273] For example, Underwager and Wakefield claimed that a study by Graesser, Woll, Kowalski, and Smith (1980) suggested that older children, when trying to revive memories, may produce more inferences, both correct and incorrect, than younger children might. Salter reviewed the study and found Underwager and Wakefield had modified the study. The researchers had actually examined college students' memories for typical and atypical actions.

Underwager and Wakefield responded to Salter's findings with a campaign of harassment including multiple lawsuits, an ethics charge, phony (and secretly taped) phone calls, and ad hominem attacks. One charge claimed Salter was laundering federal grant money. Salter refused their demands to retract her findings. The lawsuits and ethics charges against her were dismissed.

"Between the phony phone calls, the lawsuits, the ethics suits, and the slanderous (although silly) comments about laundering federal grant money," Salter wrote, "I think it is fair to state that a campaign of intimidation and harassment began against me in 1988 that lasted for several years."[274]

She challenged her colleagues. "While the multiple lawsuits and an ethics charge seemed overwhelming, who among us could, in good faith, ever face a survivor of childhood abuse again were we to run for cover when pressed ourselves? Children are not permitted that choice, and the adults who choose to work with them and with the survivors they become cannot afford to make it. It would be a choice to become, through betrayal and deceit, that to which we object."[275]

"Secrecy is the lifeblood of sexual aggression" Salter explains in *Predators: Pedophiles, Rapists, and Other Sex Offenders*. "As long as he looks and talks like us, we trust him" (p. 4). She tells parents, "Reading this book will make it harder for sex offenders to get access to you and your children."

Mark Stephenson, PhD: 1993 to 2000

Psychologist Mark Stephenson worked for an area hospital in Idaho and had a private practice. After a few clients recalled incidents of childhood sexual abuse, Idaho FMSF chapter members filed multiple complaints against him with his employer, his church, and the state licensing board. Civil suits were filed by Christopher Barden's law firm, and Stephenson was terminated from his hospital job due to the publicity from the lawsuits. Three complaints were sent to the Idaho attorney general, and Stephenson's license was suspended for a year. Stephenson declared bankruptcy. The harassment continued until 2000 when Stephenson accepted employment in another state.

David Calof: 1995 to 2005

As editor of *Treating Abuse Today* (*TAT*), Seattle therapist David Calof sent staff reporter Eva Doehr to cover a local FMSF chapter meeting. Her articles in the November/December 1994 issue coincided with the Foundation's second conference.

"Persistence pays off," the Foundation's visiting director, Pamela Freyd, told chapter members at the Seattle meeting, Doehr reported, "It took just 100 letters to get the American Medical Association to issue a cautionary statement regarding memories of abuse recovered in therapy." Her daughter had memories of abuse in order to feel better, Pam told the group.

According to attendee Phil Hoxter, "Most people come to us through Elizabeth [Loftus]. They call her first."

Chuck Noah was in Oregon the day of the meeting. "We're going to get Wendy Maltz and that cult down there [in Eugene, Oregon]," Chuck's wife, June, told the group.

The Seattle chapter compiled a "bad therapist list," and members were encouraged to add names. Attendees applauded any mention of filing complaints or lawsuits against therapists. Pam Freyd urged chapter members to write to Washington Governor Lowry and ask him to review the case of Paul Ingram, who had been accused of abuse by his daughters. Members traveled to Olympia to picket the state capitol in support of Ingram (p.14).

Doehr's second *TAT* article in the November/December issue, "The False Memory Movement's Political Agenda," described the Foundation's entry into the political arena.[276] Eric Marine with the American Professional Agency Inc. told Doehr that the Foundation had one agenda—to remove therapists from working with adult survivors of childhood sexual abuse (p. 12).

The picketing of Calof's office began in January, led by accused parent Chuck Noah. "Groups as large as 15 people set up huge displays in front of my therapy offices, sometimes stretching over three city blocks," Calof said.

Loftus's mall study co-author, Jacqui Pickrell, participated in the picketing. She attended a May 1995 conference on family mediation co-sponsored by Calof.[277] When a presenter asked the audience for questions, Pickrell rose, turned toward Calof, and angrily accused him of spreading false theories and destroying families. She questioned his right to attend the conference (personal communication, July 6, 2020).

Seattle psychologist Laura Brown, also picketed by Noah, says, "To play the role of helpless bystander disempowers and ultimately harms all of those who work for a more just world."[278]

UW psychologist Elizabeth Loftus vouched for Chuck Noah in an interview with the *Seattle Post Intelligencer*.[279] She invited him to speak to her students about his daughter's accusations. Noah accompanied her to local media appearances where he supported her from the audience.

After Calof filed anti-harassment and no-contact orders against Noah, Loftus asked the American Civil Liberties Union (ACLU) to take Noah's case.[280] The ACLU hired Seattle private investigator Scott Hatten who entered Calof's office and introduced himself, saying he was working for a man who was looking for a therapist. Calof referred him. Hatten interviewed the picketers, the business owners in the building, and Calof's wife. He sat in his car in the parking lot and aimed what Calof thought might have been a high-powered camera at Calof's office. Calof notified his clients that they may be under surveillance, a violation of their civil rights as clients.

Calof's *The Couple Who Became Each Other: Stories of Healing and Transformation from a Leading Hypnotherapist* was released in 1996. "His revealing book offers remarkable insights into the inner wisdom we all possess," Amazon says. False memory advocates picketed Calof's book readings. They fabricated stories for bookstore staff, claiming that Calof had treated them or their family members. Bantam Books backed away from promoting Calof's book. Calof says his book sold well in France, Germany, Japan, and England.

The personal attacks, harassment, and stalking by false memory proponents impacted Calof's clients, his family members, his attorney, and his attorney's family members. Calof was forced to relocate his office twice due to complaints. He shut down the publication of *Treating Abuse Today*, even though the magazine was generating a considerable profit. He estimates the harassment cost him over $1.5M in legal fees, moving expenses, and lost speaker fees. Calof says his documentation of the harassment fills 300 pages.

Following convictions for violating both an anti-harassment order and a no-contact order, Noah was convicted of stalking and fined $10,000. The conviction was upheld by the Washington State Court of appeals in 2000.[281] Noah died in 2004 following complications from diabetes.

"I cannot know whether the members and supporters of the FMSF, whom I have not examined or evaluated, have abused their children," Calof states in "Notes From a Practice Under Siege." He adds, "However, after years of unrelenting siege, I can say with certainty that many of them have abused me and innocent others connected to me, and that the FMS movement tolerates and supports this kind of *ad hominem* attack, encumbrance, and vindictiveness at the expense of reasoned dialogue."[282]

Nicole Taus Kluemper, PhD: 1997 to 2019

> "Should a psychologist intentionally breach the confidentiality of a rival theorist's case study by hiring a private investigator to gather confidential information for a competing view of the case?"
>
> **—The Leadership Council on Child Abuse & Interpersonal Violence's webpage "Trauma and Memory"**

A decade-long ethical and legal struggle began in 1997 between Nicole Taus, a nineteen-year-old freshman at the University of San Diego, and Elizabeth Loftus, a fifty-three-year-old psychology professor at the University of Washington.

Child psychiatrist David Corwin conducted a videotaped interview of then six-year-old Nicole Taus in a troubled custody case. At Taus's request, Corwin interviewed her again at seventeen with her foster mother present. During the taped interview, Taus spontaneously recalled an incident of sexual abuse by her mother.

With the permission of Taus and her father, Corwin presented the two videos at academic conferences. Respecting Taus's right to confidentiality as a case-study subject, Corwin referred to her as "Jane Doe." Corwin and psychologist Erna Olafson co-authored a "Jane Doe" case report in 1997 for *Child Maltreatment*.[283]

The videotaped, spontaneous recall of childhood trauma challenged Loftus's theory that incidents of childhood sexual abuse are implanted by therapists. Loftus set out to discredit the videos by locating Taus and investigating her personal life. A UW librarian emailed a request asking for information on the location of "a member of the armed forces named Nicole Taus."[284] Loftus and Melvin Guyer of the University of Michigan traveled to California to interview Nicole's biological mother,[285] her stepmother, and her foster mother. Nicole Taus's right to privacy as a case-study subject had ended. Documents related to the case are available at the Leadership Council's webpage "*Taus v. Loftus et al.*: Why Is This Case Important?"[286]

Taus contacted Loftus and asked her to halt contact with her family members. Loftus did not do so. Taus, by then a Navy ensign, filed an ethics complaint against Loftus with the University of Washington's Office of Scholarly Integrity (OSI) in late 1999, alleging invasion of privacy. Loftus explained to Dan Tsang at college radio station KUCI in late 2002 that her investigation of Jane Doe compared to interviews she might conduct to write an obituary.[287]

The investigation of Taus's complaint by two clinicians and a sociology professor lasted twenty-one months. Loftus was forbidden to discuss the case during the investigation. She expressed her feelings about the gag order during her acceptance speech for the William James Award. "Who, after all, benefits from my silence? Who benefits from keeping such investigations in the dark?" She answered, "My inquisitors. The only people who operate in the dark are thieves, assassins, and cowards."[288] A quote from Loftus's speech along with a political cartoon appears in *Myers' Psychology*, 8th edition, p. 389.

The ethics committee concluded in 2001 that Loftus was not guilty of the charge of scholarly misconduct, according to "The High Cost of Skepticism" by Carol Tavris. The two clinicians on the committee recommended to the dean that she be reprimanded and subjected to a program of remedial education on professional ethics. They instructed Loftus not to publish data obtained by methods they regarded as inconsistent with the "ethical principles" of psychologists.

Loftus transferred to the University of California at Irvine a year later.

UW psychology department chair Ana Marie Cauce, PhD, explained to a *Boston Globe* reporter in 2003 why the investigators faced a nearly impossible task. "On the one hand, if they are too strict, it makes it difficult for us to do our work. On the other hand, some universities have had their research funds cut off because of (human subjects) violations."[289] Cauce now serves as president of the University of Washington.

The committee's findings were subpoenaed by the defense in *Rodriguez v. Perez.*[290] Loftus's motion to quash the subpoena was denied. Loftus resigned from the case.

Taus did not receive a final report of the committee's findings.

Taus v. Loftus

Nicole Taus was attending flight school in 2002 when she was called to the operations desk. Her attorney had called. The May issue of the *Skeptical Inquirer* was on newsstands with "Who Abused Jane Doe, Part I" by Elizabeth Loftus and Melvin Guyer.[291] Part II followed in the next issue. The authors suggested "Jane Doe" had falsely accused her mother. Based on the contents of the article, Nicole determined that Loftus had not only gained access to her sealed juvenile records, but she had also interviewed her foster mother, her stepmother, and her biological mother. The authors stated that Nicole's half-brother John said there was no abuse. They failed to report he had suffered an accident as a teen that left him with severe brain damage and memory loss.

Loftus said the *Skeptical Inquirer* article gave her the satisfaction of knowing that "people will be embarrassed to use Jane Doe's case in court or in papers again," Amy Wilson with the *Orange County Register* told readers.[292]

Taus sued Loftus, Guyer, private investigator Harvey Shapiro, the University of Washington, the *Skeptical Inquirer*, and psychologist Carol Tavris[293] with invasion of privacy, fraud, and defamation. The lawsuit was appealed, and all defendants except Loftus were dropped. Taus was assessed $250,000 in legal fees accrued by the dropped defendants. Taus was a Navy helicopter pilot when the defense attorneys began garnishing her wages. The Navy frowns upon garnished wages. As a lieutenant, she made too much money to declare bankruptcy. She turned over her assets, resigned from the Navy, and declared bankruptcy.

The California Supreme Court dismissed all but one charge against Loftus—she allegedly introduced herself to Nicole's foster mother as Corwin's supervisor, someone the foster mother knew and trusted. The court's decision described the difference between what a reporter might do and what Loftus had done.[294]

> In our view, intentionally misrepresenting oneself as an associate or colleague of a mental health professional who has a close personal relationship with the person about whom one is seeking information would be a particularly serious type of misrepresentation, and one significantly different from the more familiar practice of a news reporter or investigator in shading or withholding information regarding his or her motives when interviewing a potential news source.[295]

Taus's mother submitted a declaration on July 5, 2007, stating Loftus had called her to say Nicole was "after her" and that the University was not supporting her. Loftus called her several times, telling her, "Don't talk to anyone unless I okay it."[296]

Taus made a settlement offer. The judgment would be entered in Taus's favor. Loftus would pay Taus $7,500, with each party bearing its own costs. Loftus accepted the offer. *Taus v. Loftus* settled in Taus's favor on August 28, 2007.

Two dozen reporters interviewed Loftus about the lawsuit.

Loftus edited Nicole's account for her TED Talk. "She accused her mother of sexual abuse based on a repressed memory [Nicole initially accused her as a child]. And this accusing daughter had actually allowed her story to be filmed [the two videotaped interviews] and presented in public places [at academic conferences]."[297]

Nicole Taus, now Nicole Kluemper, went on to earn a PhD in clinical psychology.

The legal documents, commentaries and articles discussing the ethics of Loftus's actions are on the Leadership Council's webpage at *Taus v. Loftus et al.*

The UW maintains a staff website for Loftus at http://staff.washington.edu/eloftus/. The website includes a link to Loftus's *Skeptical Inquirer* article on the Taus case.

Renee Fredrickson, PhD: 1992 to 2010

A reporter gave Pam Freyd a copy of the letter he received from psychologist Renee Fredrickson, author of *Repressed Memories: A Journey to Recovery from Sexual Abuse*. The letter stated, "Many established professionals who work with sexual abuse have maintained that the False Memory Syndrome Center is an organized, well-funded group of accused sexual abusers. As such, the group functions as a tool to harass, intimidate, and aggressively silence adults who have delayed memories of sexual abuse."[298]

Fredrickson was sued for malpractice in 1997 by a former client represented by attorney Chris Barden. Fredrickson denied any wrongdoing. The case settled for $175,000 in 1998.

Fredrickson described the consequences of activism for her and her family in a Nov/Dec 2011 letter to *The National Psychologist*. "My son's intro to his psychology textbook stated 'Memory Wars' was the most significant event in this era of psychology . . . My family and I have endured 19 years of stalking, harassment, professional complaints, picketing, assaults, false accusations and profane mail from false memory syndrome advocates." Fredrickson named others who were similarly harassed: David Calof, Judith Herman, Bennett Braun, and Roland Summit."

She concluded, "There should be no 'Wars' or hatred among professionals. We do not need to mimic the systems that produce victims, offenders and deniers. To do so is a grave disserve to our profession and the public."

Judith Peterson, PhD, et al.: Criminalizing Therapy

Eighteen ethics complaints and lawsuits against Houston psychologist Judith Peterson had all been settled or dismissed by October 1997. Following Peterson's two-month hospitalization for anxiety-related physical issues, a federal grand jury ruling was announced. Judith A. Peterson, PhD; Richard E. Seward, MD; George Jerry Mueck; Gloria Keraga, MD; and Sylvia Davis, MSW at Spring Shadows Glen—a mental health treatment center in Houston—were indicted on sixty counts of mail and insurance fraud for diagnosing patients with dissociative identity disorder (DID) and billing through the mail. If found guilty, the defendants faced life in prison. The Foundation informed the media:

> Dear Media Person,
>
> This is to alert you to the fact that the first CRIMINAL trial concerning "false" or "recovered" memory issues begins Tuesday, September 8 in Houston, TX.[299]

A guilty verdict may have seemed like a sure thing to US attorneys Larry D. Eastepp, Quincy L. Ollison, and W. Brad Howard. Many of the witnesses had previously appeared, unchallenged, on *Frontline*'s "The Search for Satan."

Under cross-examination by defense attorney Rusty Hardin, *Frontline* veteran Mary Shanley, the government's star witness, could not name any memory that was implanted by the staff at Spring Shadows Glen. "Former patient can't attribute false memories to therapy" the *Houston Chronicle* announced on October 8.[300]

The government's first expert, Dr. James Hudson, reportedly had some jury members smiling as he struggled to respond under cross-examination. Elizabeth Loftus resigned as an expert following Hudson's testimony. The government's presentation was in its fifth month when five jury members and alternates were dismissed. Although a jury of eleven can return a verdict and the defense agreed to continue, the government dropped all charges in March 1999.[301]

"The government tried to criminalize therapy in this trial, but they failed," Peterson summarized in *The National Psychologist*. She added, "Now that the government's case has been shown to be thoroughly and completely off base, I don't think there's much concern out there about treating this population."[302]

Peterson did volunteer work with survivors following the trial and then retired. The social-work license of Sylvia Davis expired. Richard Seward died in 2008. Psychiatrist Gloria Keraga was seeing patients in 2022. Hospital administrator Jerry Mueck went on to become the executive vice president of a real estate firm. He did not renew his real estate license in 2020.

Government witness Mary Shanley retired after working for a school district in northern Indiana.

The trial updates were still posted in January 2022 at <u>fmsfonline. org</u>.

False Memory Lawsuits Draw to a Close

The lawsuit filings against therapists slowed in the late 1990s. One reason may have been the dismissal of the *Peterson* case. Another may have been a lawsuit in North Carolina that went to trial instead of settling. Former patient Susan A. Green sued psychologist Daphne J. Timmons and psychiatrist J. W. Scott Wallace, seeking $3M in damages. Trauma experts Judith Armstrong, PhD; Richard Kluft, MD; and Richard Loewenstein, MD, provided expert testimony for the defense. The defense hired a private investigator to examine the plaintiff's claims and argued the defendants were not using "repressed memory techniques." A headline in *The Charlotte Observer* on August 20, 1998, announced, "Jurors Believe Therapists." The trial verdict marked the first loss for Christopher Barden, the Utah-based attorney who had traveled the country suing therapists and settling.

The media turned to another story in 2002: multiple-victim cases within institutions that tolerated child predators. An accusation by one adult, or perhaps two, might be dismissed as false memories. But predators in tolerant institutions can molest dozens of children. The false memory defense doesn't hold up in these cases. False memory advocates were not typically asked for their opinion.

Chapter 18

Reckonings with Tolerant Institutions

"Beyond the inherent difficulty of detecting and
preventing this most secret crime, beyond the obstacle
course of concealment erected by the collusion of clever
pedophiles, the child victims of sexual abuse are betrayed by
organizations that repeatedly prefer to avoid embarrassment
by concealing awkward allegations and by a system of
protection which simply does not work."

—Nick Davies, *The Guardian*, 1998

Our families, churches, private and public schools, gymnastic organizations, dance companies, coaching organizations, and medical facilities—all institutions where children can be found— attract predators. These predators gain access to children, and in turn, provide income and/or services to the institutions. When a child molester is reported, the institution may protect its reputation by silencing or shunning the member who made the accusation. This denial ensures the institution can maintain its reputation as a place that's safe for children.

Tolerant institutions are facilitated by bystanders who "know, but they don't know," says psychiatrist Sylvia Solinski.[303] Bystanders dismiss suspicious behavior by telling themselves, "That's just the way he is," "He contributes so much to us," "He would never do anything like that," "He just loves children," "The child looks fine, so he's not hurting them," "It's not my responsibility," "No one else is doing anything, so it must be okay." Everyone knows what they're doing to children, yet no one knows.

To Avoid Reporting

Pedophilia is "a well-known phenomenon in many clerical circles," Paul Wilkes said in "Unholy Acts" for *The New Yorker Magazine* in 1993.[304] He described what church officials might say to avoid reporting abusive priests to authorities.

1. Child molestation is not a matter of pathology or legality but of immorality—a failing. The priest-pedophile is asked to repent his sin.

2. Children are viewed as inanimate objects, as sources of temptation for a consecrated servant of God.

3. They're children—they don't know anything about sex. They forget about it.

4. A priest's innocence is presumed. To reveal a priest's shortcomings is akin to blasphemy.

5. Officials don't want to turn the church into a police state, tracking down every report of child sex abuse.

6. Reporting the priest could open up the diocese to lawsuits.

The Consequences of Not Reporting

If an institution's leadership receives a report of suspected child abuse and fails to notify authorities, the suspect has finessed the institution into becoming a coconspirator. The institution then becomes liable for damages resulting from protecting a child predator.

If the institution decides to investigate the accusation before reporting the suspect, this raises further concerns. According to the Jacob Wetterling Resource Center,

1. We are not trained to assess an allegation.

2. A delay in reporting may result in a loss of evidence or the perpetrator may pressure the child to recant.

3.   A delay is a violation of the law in most states.

4.   An untrained investigator may taint the memories.[305]

A failure to report the child molester may increase the severity of the abuse for the child, psychologist Warwick Middleton reported in an International Society for the Study of Trauma and Dissociation webinar. "As far as I can determine, the more prolonged child sexual abuse is, the more likely it is to incorporate elements of organized abuse and associated psychologically conditioned responses. Part of that conditioned response for many children is to initially reflexively deny the abuse took place."[306]

"Pope's Child Porn 'Normal' Claim Sparks Outrage among Victims" the *Belfast Telegraph* reported in 2010.[307] "This is a horrible scandal within the church, but also within the whole society," Bishop Olmstead, head of the Phoenix diocese, said when he resigned in January 2022 at seventy-five. "We have a very deep obligation as the church to reach out to these people whether they've been abused by someone in the church or somebody else in society." The bishop held biannual Masses dedicated to survivors for twenty years.

A Second Reckoning

A second reckoning with child molesters began in 2002 when *The Boston Globe* covered the story of a tolerant institution, the Catholic Church. Priests accused of molesting children were transferred to other dioceses. The new dioceses were not informed of the accusations. The priests continued to molest.

For the first time in a decade, the media failed to attend the FMS Foundation's annual (and last) conference in 2002. The media had a new story. *The Globe's* early headlines in 2002 announced, "Church Allowed Abuse by Priest for Years: Aware of Geoghan's Record, the Archdiocese Still Shuttled Him from Parish to Parish," and "Geoghan Preferred Preying on Poorer Children."

Rather than interviewing the church officials who might deny the accusations, or the false memory experts who would declare the accusations suspect, *The Globe's* "Spotlight" team dug deeper. They uncovered a pattern of pervasive child abuse within the Catholic Church that was facilitated by church officials.

"Goeghan found extraordinary solace in the church's culture of secrecy," the Spotlight team reported in *Betrayal: The Crisis in the Catholic Church*. The authors describe how Maryetta Dussourd found no support from the church when she told them Goeghan was molesting her boys. Fellow parishioners shunned her and accused her of provoking scandal (p. 18). Goeghan was eventually sent to prison. He was serving a ten-year prison sentence when he was murdered by a fellow prisoner in 2003.

TIME, Newsweek, People Magazine, and the *U.S. News and World Report* devoted forty articles to the clergy abuse story in 2002. Bishop Accountability at https://www.bishop-accountability.org/ lists the continuing media reports on priest abuse.

Priests and False Memories

Reporters ask questions and take notes when interviewing experts. Experts who testify in court proceedings are held to a higher standard. Prosecutors prepare to cross-examine experts by examining their prior research and testimony.

Former priest Paul Shanley was on trial in Boston in 2005 and facing criminal charges of child rape.[308] After years of amnesia, the key witness had recovered memories of Shanley sexually assaulting him as a child. The prosecutor did her homework. As she cross-examined Loftus, she showed how Loftus's descriptions of the Ira Hyman hospitalization study had 'changed' over time (transcript, pp. 59–64). The jury found Shanley guilty. Loftus billed $15,000 for her travel time and testimony.[309, 310]

Following the Shanley verdict, media representatives stood their ground on false memory claims. On NPR's "Day to Day," *Slate* legal analyst Dahlia Lithwick said, "Scientists have come up with the false memory syndrome," she said. "The false memories have been cooked up by negligent therapists."[311]

Psychiatrist Richard Loewenstein, medical director of The Trauma Disorders Program at Sheppard Pratt Health Systems in Baltimore, MD, responded in a letter to NPR. He described Lithwick's statements as "misinformation about the controversy over delayed recall of traumatic memories." He noted, "It was never controversial when traumatized soldiers described complex forms of amnesia for battle during the two World Wars, the Korean conflict, and the Vietnam War."[312] NPR did not respond.

Jonathan Rauch covered the Shanley story for *The Atlantic* in March 2005. He described traumatic amnesia as "quackery."[313]

JoAnn Wypijewski took a similar approach in her review of the Academy Award–winning "Spotlight" for Counterpunch: "Shanley is now imprisoned for crimes that are heinous in description and absolutely unsupported by evidence." She described as "grotesque" a brief to the International Criminal Court demanding "investigation and prosecution" of the Vatican for crimes against humanity. She added, "Liberals who cheer this sort of thing ought to ponder whether they have any principles at all, or whether those are contingent, jelly-like and poisoned by prejudice.[314]

In contrast, Maureen Orth writing for *Vanity Fair* noted the indifference of the Boston archdiocese to anything but the threat of a scandal.[315] "I came to understand what true Evil is as never before as well as the sin of pride–the pride of the Church for thinking that its reputation was more important than saving children's lives."

Washington Post executive editor Marty Baron, then *The Boston Globe*'s executive editor, commented on "Spotlight" in an interview with Karie Angell Luc for *The Quill*. "I think the most satisfying part of it is that it drew attention to the importance of investigative journalism and how investigative journalism can be practiced in the right way," he said, adding, "and what kind of impact it has and what kind of good it can do" (p. 24).

The *Shanley* decision was appealed to the Massachusetts Supreme Judicial Court in 2009. Nearly 100 false memory proponents signed an amicus brief dismissing dissociative amnesia as "pernicious psychiatric folklore devoid of convincing scientific evidence."[316]

An amicus brief from the Leadership Council on Child Abuse and Interpersonal Violence stated that the fact that child sexual abuse can cause "dissociative memory loss and recovered memory is beyond scientific dispute."[317] Shanley's appeal was denied.

Shanley was released from prison in 2017 after serving twelve years. He was on probation for ten years in Ware, Pennsylvania, where he lived with other Level 3 sex offenders.[318] He died in 2020.

Tolerant Institutions

An exhaustive, informal survey of well-known, metropolitan and national publications from September 2016 through September 2018 found nearly 800 media reports of tolerant institutions: 94 percent of the reports were pro-victim. Six percent were skeptical or pro-accused.[319]

Southern Baptist

Predators are drawn to institutions where the leadership does not respond to reports of sexual abuse. "Southern Baptist leaders routinely silenced sexual abuse survivors," *The Houston Chronicle* reported in 2022.[320] An investigation by *Guidepost Solutions* found that a small group of leaders within the church ensured that reports of sexual assault within the church were not dealt with. The leaders had compiled a list of 703 accused predators.

The Mercy Corps

The *Mercy Corps* case demonstrates how the media can uncover what an institution's leadership has covered up by claiming the accusations are false memories. Although Dr. Loftus did not testify in the case, the defendant maintained the accusations were false memories. In 1992, Tania Culver Humphrey reported years of sexual abuse by her father, Mercy Corps leader Ellsworth Culver. The organization accepted Ellsworth's contention that his daughter's accusations were false memories. Tania Culver tried again. She asked that her accusations be investigated. The organization stood by its initial assessment that there was "insufficient evidence" to support her claims. That changed after *The Oregonian* investigated the story in 2019 and quoted witnesses who corroborated details of her story. Tjada D'Oyen McKenna, the chief executive of Mercy Corps, said the organization was horrified by the revelations. The independent investigation conducted by Freeh Group International Solutions in May 2021 revealed the abuse was much more extensive than Culver had originally reported.

Tania Culver says today, "If people can feel safe enough to talk about what's happened to them and we can bring this out, it's hard and it's awful and it's terrible, but that's how things will eventually get better. It's going to save people's lives."[321]

False Memories and Celebrities

Bill Cosby and False Memories: 2016

Cosby's defense team relied on Elizabeth Loftus to review the allegations of thirteen potential witnesses. The women's memories were all "tainted in the decades since their alleged assaults occurred," Loftus concluded.[322] She was not called to testify. A jury found Cosby guilty on three counts of aggravated indecent assault.

Cosby was released in 2021. Prosecutor Bruce L. Castor Jr. had told Cosby that he would not face criminal charges if he testified in a civil trial. The subsequent criminal charge, the court stated, violated Cosby's rights by reneging on a promise not to charge him. He was released from prison.

Dr. Loftus testified for Bill Cosby in a civil suit filed by Judy Huth in 2022. A jury awarded the plaintiff $500,000.

Jerry Sandusky's False Memory Appeal: 2019

The Sandusky story is unusual in that so much has been reported to explain why so many supported him. "My first reaction was that there had been a mistake of some sort. They have the wrong man. This is a man who has been a fisher of lost souls, not a predator," sports columnist Bill Lyon said in the *Philadelphia Inquirer*.[323]

"Horsing around in the shower? That was Jerry being Jerry. It did not occur to them that the goofy, horseplaying Sandusky they thought they knew was another of Sandusky's deceptions," noted Malcom Gladwell for *The New Yorker*.

"The most damaging portion of former FBI Director Louis Freeh's comprehensive report on the Pennsylvania State pedophilia scandal is the conclusion that four senior university officials concealed Sandusky's child abuse because they wanted "to avoid the consequences of bad publicity," Bill George wrote in "Penn State Lesson: Today's

Cover-Up Was Yesterday's Opportunity." Graham Spanier, the former president of Pennsylvania State University, reported to jail in June 2021 to begin a two-month sentence for his failure to report a 2001 allegation of sexual abuse of a child by Jerry Sandusky. By failing to report, he had endangered children.

"If there is one thing we hope the citizens of Pennsylvania have learned from the Sandusky case and the Freeh report, it is that trying to protect adults rather than children allows perpetrators to victimize even more children," said Rachel Berger, PhD, and Mary Carrasco, PhD, writing for the *Pittsburgh Post-Gazette*.

In Loftus's request to testify in Sandusky's appeal, she said she would describe how false memories are developed, then point to examples in the case that might have led to false memories.

Judge John Fedora dismissed Loftus's request as "having been rendered after an uncritical review of an absurdly incomplete record carefully dissected to include only pieces of information tending to support Appellant's repressed memory theory."[324]

False Memories and Murder Charges

Loftus testified in the defense of record producer Phil Spector who was found guilty of the murder of Lana Clarkson in 2008.

She testified at $600/hour in the defense of real estate heir Robert Durst who was found guilty of the murder of Susan Berman in 2021. Deputy district attorney John Lewin's cross-examination of Loftus on days 39–41 of the trial is on YouTube at "Durst trial + Loftus."

Durst was found guilty. He died in January 2022.

Professor Blasey Ford and Supreme Court Nominee Kavanaugh: 2018

> "I think a good portion of the deference from reporters comes from a sense of vanity, where the reporter wants to seem like they Get It and are just as smart as this billionaire (or expert) they're talking to, while the rest comes from not wanting to be rude to this crucial contact."

> **—Ashley Feinberg, interview with Mathew Ingram for the**
> ***Columbia Journalism Review*, 2019**

Circuit court judge Brett Kavanaugh was nominated to the Supreme Court in 2018. Following the announcement, psychology professor Christine Blasey Ford accused Kavanaugh of sexually assaulting her as a teenager. Elizabeth Loftus, PhD, broke records for originality in her efforts to flood the media with her ideas on why Blasey Ford's accusation might be false.

CNN news anchor Anderson Cooper relied on leading questions in his interview on September 17. "Professor Loftus, when you look at the claim that Professor Blasey Ford has made, if you were involved in an investigation, what more would you want to know? I mean how reliable is a memory from 1982?"

Loftus responded, "The real question in this case that I have is . . . when did she attach the name Brett Kavanaugh to the episode that she is recounting from when she was 15 years old?"

Cooper followed up, "In a memory that old, in a traumatic incident, somebody can attach somebody's name who was not involved?"

Loftus responded, "So I think somebody ought to be investigating this case and find out, not only did this happen, which it may well have happened, but who actually did it."

Interviewed by Scott Morefield for *Townhall* on September 23, Loftus asked, "He was a nobody back then. How did she know it was him?" Loftus went on to describe the fondling she experienced as a teen following a party.

She speculated to Benedict Carey and Jan Hoffman with *The New York Times* on September 25 as to when Blasey Ford remembered the assault. "Was it right away or did it come much later, say, in therapy?"

Ford's husband's affidavit was ambiguous, Loftus told Paul Mulshine with *The Star-Ledger* on September 27. "It insinuates she said the name [of Kavanaugh] in that 2012 therapy session, but he doesn't assert it."

Some tried circuitous logic. On September 17, David French with the *National Review* repeated Loftus's comments in Julia Belluz's follow-up article to the *Rolling Stone* article covering an assault allegation at the University of Virginia.

Loftus suggested to columnist John Ziegler at *Mediaite* on September 24 that if Blasey Ford had read Mark Judge's book mentioning "Bart O'Kavanaugh," this might have planted the seed of a false memory."

On October 3, Margot Cleveland with *The Federalist* noted that Blasey Ford served as a statistical consultant for a 2008 article discussing therapeutic techniques, including hypnosis. Loftus suggested this raises "the question as to whether Ford's therapist hypnotized her."

Other experts took a different approach. Writing for the *Scientific American*, psychologist Jim Hopper, PhD, explained that *peripheral details*, what we don't pay attention to, can be distorted, but not *central details*, what we do pay attention to. What Blasey Ford paid attention to that evening is what she remembered.

Psychology Today blogger Ira Hyman, PhD, said the same. People tend to remember what they consider *central* details correctly. Blasey Ford had always remembered most, but not all, of the details.

Blasey Ford and Kavanaugh testified before the Senate Judiciary Committee on September 27. The Senate voted along party lines (50 to 48) on October 6 to confirm Kavanaugh as a Supreme Court Justice.

Senator Susan Collins voted to confirm Kavanaugh. She explained to Caroline Kelly at CNN, "I do not believe that Brett Kavanaugh was her assailant. I do believe that she was assaulted. I don't know by whom, I'm not certain when."

Blasey Ford's family was forced to leave their home following death threats. The harassment continued after Kavanaugh was confirmed. At a fundraiser hosted by Futures Without Violence, Blasey Ford said she was aware she would be attacked following her accusation. "As psychologists and sociologists, we expect that survivors of sexual assault will experience what we call DARVO. That acronym stands for denial by the accused, recast the victim as the offender."

False Memories in a Nassar-Related Case: 2018

"Larissa Boyce, now 38, and Amanda Thomashow, 29, struggle with having been called liars for so long. 'It's years of convincing yourself that you were wrong,' says Thomashow. 'You feel dirty, like you were the one who turned this completely platonic event into something sexualized.'"

—Liz Brody, The Army of Women Who Took Down Larry Nassar, *Glamour,* **2018**

Kathy Klages is reportedly the first Michigan State official informed of Nassar's crimes. Klages said she did not remember the reports when she was questioned by an investigator with the Michigan Attorney General's Office. She was charged with two counts of lying to a peace officer.

Klages's defense team relied on Elizabeth Loftus to provide expert testimony on memory. An Ingram County Circuit Court judge ruled that Loftus's testimony wasn't necessary to explain matters related to memory. The Court of Appeals declined to review the decision.

Klages was found guilty.

Simone Biles testified before the Senate Judiciary Committee in 2021, stating that the sexual abuse by Larry Nassar had a direct impact on her mental health at the 2020 Tokyo Olympic Games where she unexpectedly withdrew from several events.[325] The Justice Department's Inspector General found that FBI officials made false statements and failed to properly document complaints by the accusers.[326]

Woody Allen and False Memories: 2014, 2021

Loftus stated in *The National Law Journal*, "Memory, of course, is at the heart of the Dylan-Woody matter, since there apparently were no witnesses or any other form of corroboration to support Farrow's allegations that Allen told her to lie on her stomach in that attic and to play with an electric train set while he assaulted her."[327]

The *Allen v. Farrow* HBO documentary in 2021 presented indirect evidence corroborating Dylan Farrow's accusations—boundary violations, testimony regarding the train, Dylan's childhood interviews, etc.

Harvey Weinstein and False Memories: 2020

> "How do we explain that when we say 'Believe women,'
> we're not saying that women *never* lie—we're merely saying
> that for years we've behaved as if they *always* do. Believe
> women, rather than just defaulting to believing the men
> who claim the sex was consensual, she asked for it, she
> was wearing a skirt."
>
> **—Monica Hesse, *The Washington Post*, 2020**

Before the trial began, Jodi Kantor and Megan Twohey, along with Ronan Farrow, investigated the women's accusations in-depth and shared a Pulitzer.

Weinstein's attorneys initially announced they planned to call psychologist Deborah Davis to testify on how trauma can lead to false memories. Davis and Elizabeth Loftus co-authored "Remembering Disputed Sexual Encounters: A New Frontier for Witness Memory Research." Assistant district attorney Joan Illuzzi-Orbon argued that Davis's theories have not been accepted by the scientific community. Davis did not testify. Weinstein relied on the expert testimony of Elizabeth Loftus. She was not permitted to speculate on the testimony of the individual women who accused Weinstein.

Loftus conceded under cross-examination, "Well, if something traumatic happens, oftentimes people will remember, you know, the core of the event and maybe some core details. The peripheral details can suffer" (p. 321).

Weinstein was convicted of sex crimes and sentenced to twenty-three years. He faces charges of up to 100 years in California.

Ghislaine Maxwell and False Memories: 2021

Loftus told the jury how false memories are formed and suggested the witnesses may have formed false memories. She conceded that the central/core details, what we pay attention to, are accurate.[328]

Thirty years earlier, the Associated Press had established an editing standard indicating doubt by enclosing "repressed" in sneer quotes. In 2021 The media expressed doubt about Loftus's testimony with sneer quotes:

Reuters: Ghislaine Maxwell's Defense Calls on "False Memories" Expert in Sex Abuse Trial

BBC News: Ghislaine Maxwell Trial: "False Memory'" Expert Testifies for Defence

New York Post: Ghislaine Maxwell's Team Calls "false memories" Expert to Undermine Accusers' Claims

Amanda Darrach with the *Columbia Journalism Review* reviewed the media coverage. The transcript of the testimony of witness Annie Farmer, PhD, contained the word "boots" forty-seven times and "journal" ninety-nine times. The word "breasts" appeared eighteen times. The Associated Press did not mention "boots" or "journal," but "breasts" appeared five times. In *The New York Times* recap of the day, "boots" appeared once, "journal" twice, and "breasts" six times.[329] Maxwell was convicted of conspiracy to entice a minor to travel to engage in illegal sex acts, conspiracy to transport a minor with the intent to engage in criminal sexual activity, transporting a minor with the intent to engage in criminal sexual activity, and conspiracy to commit sex trafficking of minors.

John Sweeney with *The Guardian* summarized, "Ghislaine Maxwell's defense in New York opened with a nice lady who hadn't seen anything, a travel agent who booked flights years after they mattered and a professor of BugsBunnyology [Loftus]—and none of them cut the mustard."[330]

"Ghislaine Maxwell Was Found Guilty. But Did Survivors Get Justice?" by Julie Dahlstrom and Rachel Wechsler for *WBUR*, NPR's station in Boston, described the hurdles the witnesses faced: arduous cross-examination and privacy violations. Defense attorneys stereotyped them and suggested they lied to receive payouts from Epstein.

Chapter 19

The Foundation Shuts Down

The False Memory Syndrome Foundation underwent a gradual closing following its first decade of operation. After board member Martin Orne's death in 2000, the Foundation moved to a three-story townhouse at 1955 Locust Street in Philadelphia, a block away from the Freyd home. Income from membership dues dropped to $5,996 in 2001 and to zero by 2002. Direct public support continued, averaging $121K annually.

Foundation documents were boxed in 2009 and shipped to the Center of Inquiry in Buffalo, New York. A room was set aside to archive the documents, funded by a $100,000 donation from Samuel D. Schack and a $25,000 contribution from the Foundation. By 2011, the Foundation's address was P.O. Box 30044, and distribution of quarterly newsletters ceased. By 2015, Pamela Freyd was running the Foundation out of her home at 1900 Rittenhouse Square in Philadelphia. The Foundation website announced its closure in December 2019:

> After 27 years, the FMS Foundation dissolved on December 31, 2019. During the past quarter-century, a large body of scientific research and legal opinions on the topics of the accuracy and reliability of memory and recovered memories has evolved. People with concerns about false memories can communicate with others electronically. The need for the

FMS Foundation diminished dramatically over the years. The FMSF website and Archives will continue to be available.

Freyd's announcement failed to include the Foundation's many accomplishments.

1. They gave us two words to silence adults who disclosed childhood sex abuse: "false memories."

2. They achieved search engine optimization (SEO) so that searches for "repressed memory" generate articles that describe the memories as false.

3. They instituted widespread false memory reports in mainstream media.

4. Their false memory claims appear in psychology textbooks and in law and mental health education materials.

5. They

    - cyberbullied/harassed reporters/editors who challenged false memory claims,

    - responded to critics with litigation threats/ stalking/picketing/gaslighting,

    - asked chapter members living near an accuser to contact/stalk the accuser,

    - picketed conferences for trauma treatment providers,

    - picketed survivor conferences,

    - promoted a conference encouraging lawsuits against therapists,

    - encouraged the filing of ethics complaints against therapists,

    - encouraged the filing of lawsuits against therapists,

    - initiated efforts to charge a therapist with a

crime if a sex abuse accusation was reported during therapy,

- encouraged non-accusing family members to silence the accuser, and

- telephoned accusers' partners and encouraged them to silence the accuser.

6. They influenced the media and other organizations and

- generated an 85 percent pro-accused stance within the popular press by 1994

- promoted failed false memory research as science,

- countered claims that adult/child sexual contact is harmful to children,

- notified Ralph Nader, state Consumer Fraud Committees, and others that adults' accusations are false memories,

- generated hundreds of seemingly spontaneous letters to influence the policies of organizations and the media,

- misrepresented corroborated recovered memory cases,

- influenced psychology textbook editors to portray memory as unreliable,

- encouraged judicial rulings dismissing sex abuse allegations as false memories,

- informed psychology teachers via the APS website and the APA (TOPPS) that adults' memories of childhood sexual abuse are unreliable.

Chapter 20

False Memories in the Culture

"Children are odd little creatures. If they are badly
frightened, especially by something they don't
understand, they don't talk about it. They bottle it up.
Seemingly, perhaps, they forget it. But the memory is
still there deep down."

—Agatha Christie, *Sleeping Murders*, 1976

"Memory can cloak trauma in another 'better' narrative,
sparing us until we're ready to deal."

—Roger Ebert, review of "The Tale," 2013

Expenditures in the millions of dollars by accused parents throughout the 1990s and beyond generated hundreds of false memory mentions in political cartoons from the popular press, theater, television,
novels and psychology textbooks.

Political Cartoons

Smiling Through Tears by Pamela Freyd and Eleanor Goldstein published by SIRS Publishing in 1998 is a collection of dozens of political
cartoons satirizing therapists and survivors of child sexual abuse.

In a Doug Marlette cartoon, Pinocchio says, "I wasn't exactly
lying! I thought it was a repressed memory! But poor old Geppeto

got sent up on a morals charge." In a *Doonesbury* cartoon, Mark asks Dr. Dan Asher—described as the leading recovered memory guru—"So, Dan, how's the family?" Asher replies, "Not so good. I had to sue mom."

Some of these cartoons found their way into psychology textbooks. Weiten's *Psychology: Themes and Variations* in 2013 shows Mark from *Doonesbury* under "suggestive" hypnosis with Dr. Dan Asher who says, "You see something, don't you? It's an alien, right?"

Mark says, "Um, I don't think so."

Asher responds, "Then it's your mother. She's holding a knife, isn't she?"

David G. Meyers' *Psychology* includes a Lee Lorenz cartoon: "Under hypnosis, Mr. Morvald recovered long-buried memories of a perfectly normal, happy childhood."

A Signe Wilkinson cartoon from 1993 shows a receptionist asking a potential client "How much abuse can you afford to remember?"[331] A display board stands next to the receptionist's desk.

Dr. VIC TIMM, Psychiatrist Rates:		
$10,000		Memory of abuse by a parent
$20,000		Memory of abuse by a teacher
$30,000		Memory of abuse by a priest
Specialty Memories: Price on Request		

Asked about the cartoon, Wilkinson responded in a November 14, 2014 email, "I do remember the cartoon. It was in regard to a local case that seemed to many as false accusations. It was used elsewhere to defend the church from charges of sex abuse." Wilkinson's cartoon appeared in *The Anchor*, a Massachusetts-based Catholic journal edited by Rev. John Moore. The cartoon's appearance coincided with the 1993 sentencing of former priest James Porter to eighteen to twenty years after he pled guilty to molesting twenty-eight children in the 1960s.

Bishop Sean O'Malley called the cartoon "inappropriate and insensitive" in an *AP News* story. He apologized, saying, "I am embarrassed that such a statement would appear in a Catholic journal.

My one desire has been for healing and reconciliation."[332] The story concluded with a bow to the accused. "The American Medical Association (AMA) this year adopted a resolution saying that memory enhancement techniques in the area of childhood sexual abuse are 'fraught with problems of potential misapplication.'"[333] Notably, the AMA advisory was issued after 100 Foundation members sent letters to the organization.[334]

Artist Lynn Schirmer's cartoon in the May/June 1997 issue of *Treating Abuse Today* featured false memory "chefs" standing in the kitchen, discussing their menu for a hungry reporter: unverified false memory cases and uninvestigated stories."[335]

Television

Made-for-television movies in the early 1990s featured biographical stories of adults molested as children. *Fatal Memories* starring Shelly Long in 1992 tells the story of Eileen Franklin's recovered memories of murder.[336] *Shattered Trust: The Shari Karney Story* with Melissa Gilbert in 1993 features an attorney who recovered memories of childhood abuse. *Ultimate Betrayal* with Marlo Thomas as Sharon Simone in 1994 recounts the story of two sisters who sued their FBI father.

Television programs have addressed false memories to varying degrees. In the 2001 *Law and Order* episode "Repression" by Marilyn Osborne, a daughter's abuse allegations against her father are found to be the result of suggestion and sodium amytal when an examination shows the daughter is a virgin.

In the 2011 *Castle* episode "Demons," Jack, age eleven, witnesses a murder and represses the memory. Twenty years later, he remembers the murder and is murdered for remembering.

In the *Criminal Minds* episode "Foundation," a character says early on that a lot of women manufacture memories leading to an overuse of resources. Later in the program, memories related to a serial kidnapper of children are found to be true. In the episode "Blacklist," Liz undergoes an interrogation to unlock memories from her childhood. Within moments, she is recalling the night of a fire when she was four years old. Back in her room, she opens the box from her stepfather and finds the stuffed animal she recalled during the interrogation.

Theater

Two playwrights adopted false memory scenarios for the stage with dramatic results. In Mike Cullen's *Anna Weiss* in 1997, therapist Weiss moves in with her client to begin a lesbian relationship only to realize that her client's memories are her own. Playwright Arnold Wesker's *Denial* in 2000 closes with an enraged client whose therapist, the client says, has indoctrinated her with a "dubious creed" of child sexual abuse.

Novels

Psychiatrist Bessel van der Kolk suggests that, just as recollections of abuse must make sense within the framework of the client's history, a character's memories of abuse must make sense within the framework of a novel.[337] Unlike television, novels permit the reader to pause and ask, "Docs this make sense?" Nearly three dozen novelists have relied upon recovered memories of childhood sexual abuse as a plot device that works. Characters are initially shocked and horrified by what they recall. Then they proceed to make sense of their life based on what they've recalled. Two of these novels are described below. Others are listed at www.lynncrook.com.[338]

A Thousand Acres by Jane Smiley, 1991

An Iowa farmer's decision to divide his farm between his three daughters sets off a chain of events that brings dark truths to light. The father sexually abused two of the three daughters; one always remembered.

All Around the Town by Mary Higgins Clark, 1993

Kidnapped and sexually abused as a child, Laurie comes to believe (incorrectly) that her alter committed a murder.

The Pulitzers

Nigel Jaquiss at the *Willamette Week* received a Pulitzer in 2005 for his investigation exposing former governor Neil Goldschmidt's sexual misconduct with a teenage girl.

When the media began investigating institutions that tolerate child molesters, the Pulitzer Prize Board took notice. *The Boston Globe*'s "Spotlight" team received the Pulitzer in Public Service in 2003 for its investigation of the Catholic Church's tolerance of predator priests. The film "Spotlight," based on the investigation, received an Academy Award for Best Picture in 2016.

A Pulitzer went to Sara Ganim at *The Patriot-News* in 2012 for her story on the child sex abuse scandal involving Penn State's tolerance of crimes committed by football coach Jerry Sandusky. Ganim reported she was attacked on social media by Sandusky's supporters.[339]

The Salt Lake Tribune staff received a Pulitzer in 2017 for its reporting on the "perverse, punitive and cruel" treatment accorded to those victimized at Brigham Young University.[340]

Jodi Kantor, Megan Twohey, Emily Steel, and Michael S. Schmidt at *The New York Times* received the 2018 Pulitzer Prize for Public Service for their #MeToo reporting on Hollywood's tolerance of one of its most influential producers, Harvey Weinstein. They shared the award with Ronan Farrow at *The New Yorker*.

The Washington Post staff received the Pulitzer in 2018 for Investigative Reporting after investigating decades-old allegations of sexual misconduct by Roy Moore, a Senate candidate and former chief justice of the Supreme Court of Alabama.

While the *Indy Star* did not receive a Pulitzer for its coverage of Larry Nassar, Marisa Kwiatkowski, Mark Alisia, Steve Berta, Tim Evans, and Robert Scheer received an American Society of News Editors Award, the O'Brien Fellowship Award, and a Newseum award for their work leading to over 400 women coming forward to report molestation by Nassar at Michigan State.

A Pulitzer for Investigative Reporting in 2019 went to Matt Hamilton, Harriet Ryan, and Paul Pringle at the *Los Angeles Times* for their coverage of the University of Southern California's tolerance of a gynecologist accused of violating hundreds of young women for more than a quarter-century.

In 2020, Mary F. Calvert, a freelancer for *The New York Times*, was a finalist for her photos of male sexual assault survivors in the US Army. *Pittsburgh Post-Gazette* staff were finalists that year for their investigation of sexual abuse in the Amish and Mennonite communities.

Psychology Textbooks

> "One thing I retained from my introductory psychology class was that memory, which I believed was somewhat permanent, is unreliable."

—A student, *The Michigan Daily*, 2019

> "Judging by the content of the most popular introductory psych textbooks in America, it seems likely these students are getting a highly distorted view of the field."

—Warne, R. T., Astle, M. C. & Hill, J. C., "What Do Undergraduates Learn About Human Intelligence? An Analysis of Introductory Psychology Textbooks," 2018

Psychology textbooks assure future parents, jury members, teachers, attorneys, church and family members, and victims of sexual abuse that we cannot trust our memory. Our memories aren't like videotapes, they say. The false memory story in two textbooks in 1994, coincided with the failure of the mall study that same year. The Coon textbook told students that memories of abuse are easily implanted. The Zimbardo and Weber textbook assured students that "false memory syndrome" was a valid means of determining that sex abuse allegations are false.[341]

Those who have not signed up for a psychology class may be better informed about memory than students who have taken the class, say psychologists Chris Brewin, Bernice Andrews, and Laura Mickes. Their knowledge is more consistent with the latest research. "There is no reason to abandon the old consensus about memory being malleable but essentially reliable," the authors say.[342]

Textbook Surveys

Textbooks fail to inform students that the impact of childhood trauma is generally long-term and that memories of childhood trauma can be corroborated. Psychologists Elizabeth Letourneau and Tonya Lewis surveyed twenty-four introductory psychology textbooks in 1999.[343] Four failed to mention child sexual abuse. Four informed students that childhood abuse cannot be forgotten. Memories of abuse are easily implanted, according to eight textbooks. Three informed students that "false memory syndrome" is a valid diagnosis.[344] They failed to tell students that the Diagnostic and Statistical Manual of Mental Disorders does not support the syndrome as a diagnosis.

The Myers textbook scored highest on false memory overgeneralizations. The David and Carol Myers Foundation donated $1M in 2004 to the American Psychological Society (APS) Fund for Teaching and Public Understanding of Psychological Science. Half the attendees at Myers's organizational meeting had published articles supporting childhood trauma as false memories.[345]

Subsequent introductory textbook surveys reported similar results, including Gleaves in 2007[346] and two in 2014: Kissee, Isaacson, and Miller-Perrin[347] and Brand and McEwen.[348]

Psychologist Bethany Brand and researcher Linda McEwen examined three top-selling introductory textbooks: *Myers' Psychology* (2013), Weiten's *Psychology: Themes and Variations* (2013), and Hockenbury and Hockenbury's *Psychology* (2013). The authors found the textbooks fail to address the body of research covering the impact of childhood trauma on attachment; the limbic and HPA1 systems; gene activation; and the ability to regulate emotions, impulses, and social relationships. The authors suggest that psychology students may be less effective in careers dealing with the impact of trauma, such as becoming teachers, law enforcement, health care workers, or therapists.

Recent textbooks show little change. "Most children growing up under adversity are resilient, they withstand the trauma and become well-adjusted adults (p. 137)," Myers and DeWall (2019) insist in *Exploring Psychology*, 11th edition. They cite no research to support this claim.

The Weiten textbook, 9th edition, devotes a four-inch-long story to "Support for Recovered Memories," and twenty-two inches to "Skepticism Regarding Recovered Memories" (pp. 295–297). On page 297 of this textbook, a 1994 *Doonesbury* cartoon shows Mark undergoing "on-air repressed memory therapy." Weiten fails to explain to students that repressed memory therapy is not a therapeutic approach. It's a form of defense used if an accuser has sought therapy and makes an accusation of childhood abuse.

The Hockenbury and Nolan textbook (2018) reports the results of an online survey by *Slate* magazine. Participants received four photos of political events. They were asked to report what they remembered about each photo, then asked to choose the false photo. The percentages of those who correctly chose the false political event were

- Bush with Clemens: 15 percent,
- Lieberman impeachment vote: 15 percent,
- Obama with Ahmadinejad: 26 percent, and
- Hilary Clinton ad: 36 percent.

Although the authors suggest their findings show that memories were implanted, the results may also suggest that we do not keep track of politicians' activities.

Despite the growing body of research confirming the impact of childhood trauma, false memory proponents denying those claims are contributing textbook authors. Examples include Richard J. McNally writing for the *Oxford Textbook of Psychopathology*, 3rd ed.; Steven J. Lynn, Scott O. Lilienfeld, Harald Merckelbach, and Timo Giesbrecht writing for *Adult Psychopathology and Diagnosis*, 7th ed.; and Steven J. Lynn, Scott O. Lilienfeld, Harald Merckelbach, and Timo Giesbrecht writing for *Psychopathology: Foundations for a Contemporary Understanding*, 4th ed.

A survey of mental health professionals in 2019, prior to a training in trauma treatment, found 68 percent felt inadequately trained to assess trauma and 75 percent felt inadequately trained to treat trauma.[349]

Psychologist Elizabeth Loftus was interviewed by a member of the American Psychological Association Teachers of Psychology in

Secondary Schools (TOPSS) in August 2020. A student called in during the interview to say she was being accused of lying about a sexual assault. Loftus corrected the student. She said she doesn't say "lie." She uses "mistaken." The caller was mistaken about the sexual assault.[350]

Conclusion

"Sexual abuse of children is a crime that our society abhors
in the abstract, but tolerates in reality."

—**S. Sgroi**, *Sexual Assault of Children and Adolescents*, 1978

Our willingness to protect our children from child molesters has been
a long journey, edging closer each decade to ensuring our children's
safety. The journey began nearly fifty years ago when the Child
Abuse Prevention and Treatment Act encouraged states to criminalize adult/child sexual contact and establish mandated reporting laws.
Efforts continued in 1988 as states lifted the statute of limitations
and allowed adults molested as children to sue for damages.

We detoured in the 1990s as accused child molesters invested millions in a campaign to convince the public, academia, and the legal
community that adults' child sex abuse allegations are false memories.

We moved forward once again in 2002 as the media investigated
multi-victim cases within institutions that tolerate child molesters.

Following the closure of the FMS Foundation in December 2019,
false memory claims are facing media challenges. Recent articles
include Katie Heaney's "The Memory War" in *New York Magazine*,
Josh Kendall's "The False Memory Syndrome at 30: How Flawed
Science Turned into Conventional Wisdom" for *Mad in America*,
and "Forgotten Memories of Traumatic Events Get Some Backing
from Brain-Imaging Studies" in *Scientific American*.

Survivors and professionals described the negative impact of false memory claims on survivors and on the field of psychology in (1) *Trauma and Memory: The Science and the Silenced*[351] and (2) "The Science and Politics of False Memories,"[352] a special issue of the *Journal of Trauma and Dissociation*.

I leave readers with these questions:

1. **Evidence**

   We've heard for nearly thirty years that the lost-in-a-mall study with older relatives confirming the subject got lost suggests that therapists can convince clients they were molested as children.

   Q: Based on the study's original result, no false memories were implanted. If researchers cannot implant memories of getting lost in their subjects, what are the chances that a therapist has implanted a memory of sexual assault in a family member who tells you she was molested as a child?

2. **A Crime?**

   Q: If an individual or an institution benefits in some way from tolerating a child molester, are they trafficking the child?

3. **Professional Disguises**

   Q What are some professions that predators might select because no one would ever suspect a _____ would molest a child?

4. **True or False**

   Q: If someone we know is accused of sexual abuse, should we decide if they are innocent or guilty? If so, on what grounds should we base our decision?

5. **Repression vs. False Memories**

   Law professor Alan Scheflin and psychologist Daniel

Brown reviewed twenty-five studies and found that all twenty-five determined that amnesia for childhood sex abuse is a common finding among a portion of adults traumatized as children.[353]

Q: Do you think that a child who is molested by someone they love, and is threatened with serious consequences if they tell, can learn to "archive" the memories?

6. **Disclosing Abuse**

Q. What should an adult who was molested as a child expect to hear when they tell a friend or family member about the abuse?

7. **Reporting**

Q. What might cause you to suspect that a child is being molested? Does it make sense to address suspicious behavior, or is it better not to interfere, not to stir up trouble? See substantiated reports of child abuse by state in Appendix.

8. **The Mathematics of Molestation**

Q. 48 million adults were molested as children. Less than 20% of those cases are reported—14% of those who are reported end up in prison. We tolerate these mathematics of child molestation. Would survivors feel less shame and embarrassment if they knew they were one of millions? Could 48 million become a voting bloc? What else could they do as a bloc?

Endnotes

CHAPTER 1

1 Ronan Farrow writes in *Catch and Kill* that as he encouraged Weinstein's victims to go public, he was reminded of what he said when his sister wanted to revive her allegations of sexual assault against Woody Allen. "I don't see why you can't just move on" he told her (p. 190).

CHAPTER 2

2 My siblings said they weren't told about this incident.

CHAPTER 3

3 Online at http://legalschnauzer.blogspot.com/2012/03/new-york-mets-pitcher-reveals-that-he.html

4 Davis quote at "Awful truths: Telling the world about incest hurts - and heals at the same time." *Chicago Tribune*, Nov. 3, 1991, p. 3.

5 1981 report at https://library.childwelfare.gov/cwig/ws/library/docs/gateway/Blob/12686.pdf?r=1&rpp=-10&upp=0&w=+NA-TIVE%28%27IPDET+PH+IS+%27%27nis-1%27%27%27%29&m=3&order=+NATIVE%28%27year%2Fdescend%27%29

6 As far as I know, my father did not molest our children when we left them in my parents' care.

7 For more on mothers who know see "The Family Secret" (1988) from *In the Heat of the Night*.

CHAPTER 4

8 Caspar, E., Loumpa, K., Keysers, C., and Gazzola, V. (2020, Nov.) Obeying orders reduces vicarious brain activation towards victims' pain. *NeuroImage*.

9 https://beaconhouse.org.uk/wp-content/uploads/2020/02/Dissociation-in-Children-Teens-Resource_compressed.pdf

10 Knight's essay is online at https://tinyurl.com/t9jbxyww.

11 Hall made this comment to me backchannel in 2021 after I asked her about a similar comment she made on a listserv.

12 *The Child Survivor—Healing Developmental Trauma and Dissociation*

13 http://www.washingtonpost.com/blogs/she-the-people/wp/2014/11/13/27365/

14   Grimes article online at https://rewire.news/article/2014/02/04/make-believe-survivor-childhood-sexual-abuse/

15   http://www.missamericabyday.com/

CHAPTER 5

16   After the judge ruled in my favor, I submitted a brief note on the decision to UW ALUMNOTES. The editor deleted the mention that Loftus had testified for the defense.

17   See: http://community.seattletimes.nwsource.com/archive/?-date=19920813&slug=1507215

CHAPTER 6

18   85% prevalence of media coverage of child sex abuse reports as false memories at https://www.researchgate.net/publication/249985363_Culture_and_the_Politics_of_Signification_The_Case_of_Child_Sexual_Abuse

19   Dylan at https://mobile.twitter.com/ELLEmagazine/status/1359497243397677056

20   20 studies at https://pages.uoregon.edu/dynamic/jjf/suggestedrefs.html

21   Cheit archive at http://blogs.brown.edu/recoveredmemory/case-archive/ www.recoveredmemory.org

22   Dalenberg's research at http://heinonline.org/HOL/Landing-Page?handle=hein.journals/jpsych24&div=21&id=&page=

23   https://www.acf.hhs.gov/cb/resource/child-maltreatment-2018.

24   Ofshe's "Life with Father" at https://www.google.com/books/edition/Making_Monsters/flCfr4CjKP8C?hl=en&gbpv=1&dq=%22Life+with+father%22+Ofshe&pg=PA123&printsec=frontcover#v=onepage&q=%22Life%20with%20father%22%20Ofshe&f=false

25   Ross E. Cheit DOI: 10.1207/s15327019eb0802_4, Consider this Skeptics of Repressed Memories, *Ethics & Behavior*, Volume 8, Issue 2 June 1998, pages 141–160.

26   Katy Butler at http://www.katybutler.com/author/articles/did-daddy-really-do-it/

27   My response to Ofshe's article in the *Journal of Child Sexual Abuse* at http://blogs.brown.edu/recoveredmemory/files/2010/09/arch_legal_crook3.pdf

28   Loftus's false memory version of Crook v. M. online at https://www.psychologytoday.com/articles/199501/its-magical-its-malleable-its-memory

29   A local reporter who interviewed Loftus told me that she refers to Crook v. M. as "The Anus Case."

30   https://blogs.brown.edu/recoveredmemory/files/2015/05/Loftus_Pickrell_PA_95.pdf

31   Detailed discussion of Loftus's resignation at https://tinyurl.com/yc4o4w52

32   Niemark editorial at https://www.psychologytoday.com/articles/199605/dispatch-the-memory-war

33   Hoffman, D. H., Carter, D. J., Viglucci Lopez, C. R., Benzmiller, H. L., Guo, A. X., Latifi, S. Y., & Craig, D. C. (2015b, September 4). *Independent review relating to APA ethics guidelines, national security interrogations, and torture* (Rev. ed.). Retrieved from https://www.apa.org/independent-review/revised-report.pdf, p. 484, footnote.

34   Award at https://search.proquest.com/openview/dfa09b1639afbe7d4687dbd0ff2c84e8/1?pq-origsite=gscholar&cbl=60929

35   Letter at http://www.nytimes.com/1995/03/26/books/l-repressed-memory-and-rules-of-evidence-250195.html

36   Comments at WITCHHNT, a listserv for false memory advocates started in 1994 and maintained by Jonathan Harris at Massachusetts Institute of Technology (MIT) in the Chemical Engineering Department.

CHAPTER 7

37   Marriage at Theo Bikel's Wiki page.

38   Sauer, M. (1995, April 11). Repressed memory care a 'war zone.' TV Datebook, *San Diego Herald-Tribune*, p. F-10.

39   The Making of a Morass: Divided Memories and Media Manipulation, *Treating Abuse Today*, May/June 1995.

40   Frontline's ethical guidelines forbid false program content. http://www.pbs.org/wgbh/pages/frontline/about-us/journalistic-guidelines/

41   Burdened by the legal, and emotional costs of harassment by false memory advocates, Calof ceased publication of *Treating Abuse Today* before the Bikel interview could be published.

42   Updated reviews of "The Search for Satan" at http://astraeasweb.net/politics/smoke.html and https://tinyurl.com/y8qv5t5v

CHAPTER 8

43   Loftus, E. (1994, January 24). Deposition of Elizabeth Loftus in the matter of Crook v. Murphy. No. 91-2-01102-5 In the Superior Court of the State of Washington, County of Benton, p. 324.

44   Coan, J. (1993, August). Creating False Memories. Senior Paper, Psychology Honors Program, University of Washington.

45 Coan's account at https://www.researchgate.net/profile/James-Coan/publication/11693894_Lost_in_a_Shopping_Mall_An_Experience_With_Controversial_Research/links/09e41502c0c79b4c8f000000/Lost-in-a-Shopping-Mall-An-Experience-With-Controversial-Research.pdf

46 https://blogs.brown.edu/recoveredmemory/files/2015/05/Loftus_Pickrell_PA_95.pdf

47 Australian psychologist Martha Dean, PhD, co-authored the *Ethics & Behavior* article when she was in remission from cancer. We emailed our drafts back and forth until, at draft #18, we decided our article was done. Martha died in 2000 following the publication of our article. I suspect she'd be telling me today, "I told you, Lynn, to follow everything as far it will go. And look what you discovered!" Thank you, Martha.

48 The false stories included true details. The authors describe "partial" on page 722 as subjects who wondered if they got lost, then apparently decided they didn't or they would have been reported as "implanted."

49 Loftus's response to Crook & Dean at https://www.researchgate.net/publication/11693702_Lost_in_the_Mall_Misrepresentations_and_Misunderstandings

50 Email on June 18, 2012.

51 https://business.rice.edu/wisdom/word-watch/why-it-so-convincing-repeat-a-claim-even-if-it-is-untrue

52 I conducted a comedy improv workshop at a conference, "Courage Your Name is Comedy Improv.' Attendees diagnosed with DID signed up. They were amazingly funny, natural comedians.

53 Crook & McEwen at https://www.tandfonline.com/doi/full/10.1080/15379418.2019.1601603

54 Blizard & Shaw at https://www.tandfonline.com/doi/abs/10.1080/15379418.2019.1590285?journalCode=wjcc20

55 The conference schedule stated speakers would be taped. Loftus announced her talk would not be taped.

56 Jack Jodell, "Great Progressive Voices (Part II)," *The Saturday Afternoon Post*, May 9, 2011. https://jackjodell53.wordpress.com/2011/05/09/great-progressive-voices-part-ii/.

CHAPTER 9

57 John J. O'Connor, "TV: 'Amelia' on ABC a Movie About Incest" The New York Times, January 9, 1984. https://www.nytimes.com/1984/01/09/arts/tv-amelia-on-abc-a-movie-about-incest.html.

58 Richard T. Pienciak, "America's Dirty Little Secret," "Pedophilia—Part I," *Gettysburg Times*, September 19, 1984. https://news.google.com/newspapers?id=T6oyAAAAIBAJ&sjid=hOg-

FAAAAIBAJ&pg=1641,4057689&dq=dirty-little-secret+sex-+abuse&hl=en.

59 Spider-man and Power Pack "Secrets" [Produced in Cooperation with the National Committee for Prevention of Child Abuse] (Vol. 1, No. 1, 1984)

60 Lois Timnick, "The Times Poll: 22% in Survey Were Child Abuse Victims," *Los Angeles Times*, August 25, 1985. https://www.latimes.com/archives/la-xpm-1985-08-25-mn-24801-story.html.

61 (1) John Briere & Marsha Runtz. University males' sexual interest in children: Predicting potential indices of pedophilia in a nonforensic sample. *Child Abuse & Neglect*, 13(1), 1989, 65 75. (2) Smiljanich, K., & Briere, J. (1996). Self-reported sexual interest in children: Sex differences and psychosocial correlates in a university sample. Violence and Victims, 11, 39-50. Notes online at: http://www.mhamic.org/sources/smiljanich&briere.htm (3) Freund, K. & Costell, R. (1970). The structure of erotic preference in the nondeviant male. Behavior Research and Therapy, 8, 15-20. 50% showed penile response to female children age 4–10. (4) Hall, G., Hirschman, R. and Oliver, L. (1995). Sexual arousal and arousability to pedophilic stimuli in a community sample of normal men. Behavior Therapy, 26, 681-694. 20% self-reported pedophilic interest, 26% exhibited arousal to pedophilic stimuli that equaled or exceeded arousal to adult stimuli. (5) Gordon C. Nagayama, Richard Hirschman, & Lori L. Oliver. Sexual arousal and arousability to pedophilic stimuli in a community sample of normal men. Behavior Therapy, 26(4), Fall 1995, 681-94.

62 "Actions Based on Childhood Sexual Abuse," *RCW 4.16.340*, "Title 4", "RCWs," Washington State Legislature. https://app.leg.wa.gov/rcw/default.aspx?cite=4.16.340.

63 *Barton v. Peters*, no. 4FA-90-0157, Superior Court for the State of Alaska, Fourth Judicial District, (1990): 43.

64 "State Civil Statutes of Limitations in Child Sexual Abuse Cases," "Human Services," NSCL, last modified May 30, 2017. https://www.ncsl.org/research/human-services/state-civil-statutes-of-limitations-in-child-sexua.aspx.

65 Elizabeth F. Loftus, "The Reality of Repressed Memories," Elizabeth F. Loftus, University of Washington. https://staff.washington.edu/eloftus/Articles/lof93.htm.

66 DNA was unavailable for another twenty years.

67 Joyce Wadler, "Exhuming the Horror," "Archive," *People 36*, no. 17, last modified November 4, 1991. https://people.com/archive/exhuming-the-horror-vol-36-no-17/.

68   "Old Memory Leads to a Murder Trial," *The New York Times*,
      October 25, 1990. https://www.nytimes.com/1990/10/25/us/old-
      memory-leads-to-a-murder-trial.html.

69   https://law.justia.com/cases/federal/appellate-courts/
      F3/312/423/608793/

70   Wadler, "Exhuming the Horror."

71   M. Dunlop, "Playing Tricks with Your Memory," *Toronto Star*,
      February, 1991, 2-C.

72   "Truth or Invention: Exploring the Repressed Memory Syn-
      drome; Excerpt from 'The Myth of Repressed Memory,'" *Cos-
      mopolitan* 218, no. 4, April 1995, 248. https://staff.washington.
      edu/eloftus/Articles/Cosmo.html.

73   Emma Bryce, "False Memories and False Confessions: The
      Psychology of Imagined Crimes," *Wired*, last modified July
      22, 2017. https://www.wired.co.uk/article/false-memory-syn-
      drome-false-confessions-memories.

74   "George Thomas Franklin, Plaintiff-Appellant v. Jim Fox; Martin
      Murray; Robert Morse; Bryan Cassandro; John Cuneo, Sergeant;
      Eileen Franklin-Lipsker, Defendents-Appellees, 312 F.3d 423,"
      "2002," "Ninth Circuit," "Court of Appeals," "Federal Courts,"
      "Case Law," "US Law," Justia. https://law.justia.com/cases/feder-
      al/appellate-courts/F3/312/423/608793/.

75   Holly Watt, "'Some Days I Think I Was Molested, Others I'm
      Not Sure': Inside a Case of Repressed Memory," *The Guardian*,
      September 23, 2017. https://www.theguardian.com/science/2017/
      sep/23/inside-case-of-repressed-memory-nicole-kluemper.

76   Chris Woolston, "Making the Case Against Memories As Ev-
      idence," "Society," *Knowable Magazine*, October 25, 2017.
      https://knowablemagazine.org/article/society/2017/mak-
      ing-case-against-memories-evidence.

77   "George Franklin"; Other California DNA Exonerations; The
      National Registry of Exonerations; University of California
      Irvine Center for Science & Society, University of Michigan Law
      School & Michigan State University College of Law; accessed
      May 14, 2022. https://www.law.umich.edu/special/exoneration/
      Pages/casedetail.aspx?caseid=3221.

78   "FMS Foundation Newsletter," August 1993.

79   Sandra Dee at http://www.bobbydarin.net/liveagain.html

80   "Marylyn Van Derbur Tells More of Her Story," TEDI BEAR
      Children's Advocacy Center, YouTube, https://www.youtube.
      com/watch?v=2En9O14SGyk.

81   Mary Knight, *Am I Crazy? My Journey to Determine If My
      Memories Are True*, Mary Knight Productions, 2016, http://
      maryknightproductions.com/index.html.

82 "Satanic Ritual Abuse Survivor Interviews Prof. Loftus," *REAL-WOMEN/REALSTORIES*, YouTube, November 2022. https://www.youtube.com/watch?v=lwIuG4g2QiI. You may also be interested in Loftus's video: "Satanic Child Abuse Claims Are Based on False Memories," *REAL WOMEN/REAL STORIES*, YouTube, October 2022. https://www.youtube.com/watch?v=zSbcb3_QgsQ.

83 See "Satanic Ritual Abuse Survivor" at *REALWOMEN/RE-ALSTORIES*.

84 "Hotline Usage Spikes Following Mackenzie Phillips' Interview with Oprah," Rainn, September 24, 2009, https://www.rainn.org/news/hotline-usage-spikes-following-mackenzie-phillips-interview-oprah.

85 Kirthana Ramisetti, "AnnaLynne McCord Reveals She Was Suicidal After Childhood Abuse, Sexual Assault: 'It's Time to Talk About the Truth,'" *Daily News*, May 29, 2014. https://www.nydailynews.com/entertainment/gossip/annalynne-mccord-opens-abuse-rape-article-1.1810337.

CHAPTER 10

86 David Finkelhor et al., "The Lifetime Prevalence of Child Sexual Abuse and Sexual Assault Assessed in Late Adolescence," *Journal of Child and Adolescent Health* 55 (2014): 329–333. http://www.unh.edu/ccrc/pdf/9248.pdf.

87 *Lolita* by Vladimir Nabokov (1958) was partially inspired by the real-life kidnapping of Sally Horner, who was imprisoned for two years.

88 J. Mitchell, "Memories of a Disputed Past," *The Portland Oregonian*, August 8, 1993.

89 Intracervical insemination is done with a syringe, not a turkey baster.

90 Katy Butler, "Marshalling the Media," Psychotherapy Networker, March/April 1995. http://www.katybutler.com/publications/psychnetorg/index_files/psychthernet_marshallmedia.htm.

91 Alexandra Petri, "There's Nothing Wrong with Good, Harmless Fun!" Opinion, *The Washington Post*, September 16, 2019. https://www.washingtonpost.com/opinions/2019/09/16/theres-nothing-wrong-with-good-harmless-fun/.

92 Jane Doe*, "How Could This Happen? Coping with a False Accusation of Incest and Rape," *Institute for Psychological Therapies* 3, (1991). http://www.ipt-forensics.com/journal/volume3/j3_3_3.htm#en0. *Jane Doe was identified as Pamela Freyd.

93 Stephen Fried, "War of Remembrance," originally published in *Philadelphia Magazine*, January 1994, now available on The Stacks Reader, http://www.thestacksreader.com/war-of-remembrance/.

94   "Peter J. Freyd, PhD," Fall 2018 Newsletter of the University of Pennsylvania, Education, Who's Who Newsletters, https://whoswhonewsletters.com/2019/01/04/peter-freyd/.

95   A Freyd family member provided information about Peter's summer with Conti.
Conti's murals are at http://www.uri.edu/quadangles/news-views/historic-murals-discovered-in-edwards-hall/

96   Dave Lavallee, "Historic Murals Discovered in Edwards Hall," *Quadangles Online: URI Alumni Magazine*, The University of Rhode Island, October 8, 2010. https://web.uri.edu/quadangles/historic-murals-discovered-in-edwards-hall/.

97   "FMS Foundation Newsletter," November 3, 1993—Vol. 2, No. 10, Newsletter Archives, False Memory Syndrome Foundation. http://www.fmsonline.org/newsletters/fmsf_1993_nov_v2_n10.pdf.

98   Sylvia Fraser, "Abuse Wars: Whose Memory Matters? Betrayal Trauma: The Logic of Forgetting Childhood Abuse," *Globe and Mail*, January 25, 1997, D-14 (English).

99   Jennifer Freyd and Pamela Birrell, *Blind to Betrayal: Why We Fool Ourselves; We Aren't Being Fooled* (Hoboken, New Jersey: John Wiley & Sons, Inc., 2013).

100   Dunlop, "Playing Tricks."

101   J. Hunt, "Just Memories: Psychologist States the Case Against 'Infallible' Witnesses," *Seattle Post-Intelligencer*, May 2, 1991.

102   Malcolm Ritter, "Long-Forgotten Memories Now Being Recounted in Court," *The Free Lance-Star*, May 29, 1991. https://news.google.com/newspapers?id=p9QQAAAAIBAJ&sjid=wIsDAAAAIBAJ&pg=3799,412243&dq=elizabeth-loftus+1991&hl=en.

103   Camille B. Wortman, Elizabeth F. Loftus, and Wendy Dunn, *Psychology* (New York City: Knopf, 1981): 203.

104   Tracy Thompson, "Delayed Lawsuits of Sexual Abuse on the Rise: Alleged Victims Base Legal Actions on Memories Critics Say May Be Implanted in Therapy," *The Washington Post*, August 14, 1991. https://takeback.scholarslab.org/items/show/1314.

105   Irene Wielawski, "Column One: Unlocking the Secrets of Memory: Recent Tales of Child Abuse Have a Twist—Victims, Now Adults, Say Their Memories of the Horrors Were Repressed for Decades. Critics Speak of Fantasy and Distortion," *Los Angeles Times*, October 3, 1991. https://www.latimes.com/archives/la-xpm-1991-10-03-mn-4413-story.html.

106   Coan, "An Experience with Controversial Research."

107   University City Mall in Spokane ran between Rosauers and The Crescent with shops along a single hallway. Pia Hallenberg, "University City Mall Demolition Underway," *The Spokes-*

man-Review, April 25, 2015. https://www.spokesman.com/stories/2015/apr/25/university-city-mall-demolition-underway/.

108   Coan, "Creating False Memories," 16.

109   Elizabeth F. Loftus, "You Must Remember This . . . or Do You? How Real Are Repressed Memories?" *The Washington Post*, June 27, 1993. https://www.washingtonpost.com/archive/opinions/1993/06/27/you-must-remember-this-or-do-you-how-real-are-repressed-memories/2ad65442-1a9c-4178-80df-f67f436932e9/.

110   Loftus described Coan's failure to convince his mother in her presentation "The Reality of Repressed Memory" at the APA's August 14–18 conference in Washington DC.

CHAPTER 11

111   "FMS Foundaton Newsletter," August/September, 1992 - Vol. 1, No. 8, Newsletter Archives, False Memory Syndrome Foundation. http://www.fmsfonline.org/newsletters/fmsf_1992_augsept_v1_n8.pdf.

112   Finkelhor, D. (1994). Current information on the scope and nature of child sexual abuse. *Future of Children*, 4(2), 31-53. ALSO SEE: Adverse Childhood Experiences and Adult Health (ACE) 22% of 17,421 health plan members molested as children. (Extrapolate: 50 million adults) http://xnet.kp.org/permanente-journal/winter02/goldtolead.html

113   "FMS Foundation Newsletter," June 1992.

114   U.S. Department of Health & Human Services, Administration for Children and Families, Administration on Children, Youth and Families, Children's Bureau. (2022). Child Maltreatment 2020. (Table 3-2) Available at https://www.acf.hhs.gov/cb/data-research/child-maltreatment

115   Joshua Kendall, "Forgotten Memories of Traumatic Events Get Some Backing from Brain-Imaging Studies," *Scientific American*, April 6, 2021. https://www.scientificamerican.com/article/forgotten-memories-of-traumatic-events-get-some-backing-from-brain-imaging-studies/.

116   *The Kansas City Star* covered the story of Janet Curry, who publicly accused her father, the former Jackson County presiding judge Charles E. Curry, of incest. In turn, her father scheduled a televised press conference. He denied the accusations publicly and demanded an accounting from the church that had provided the room where his daughter spoke (July 1992).

117   Mark Kind, "Repressed Memories," *The Pitch*, January 10, 2002. https://www.thepitchkc.com/repressed-memories/.

118   DHHS data in 1981 listed 44,700 reports of childhood sexual abuse. Substantiated reports averaged 42.7% (p. 11). Nearly half

the mothers had tolerated the abuse of their children (p. 32). Lisa Jones and David Finkelhor, "The Decline in Child Sexual Abuse Cases, *Juvenile Justice Bulletin*, Office of Juvenile Justice and Deliquency Prevention, US Department of Justice, January 2001. https://www.ojp.gov/pdffiles1/ojjdp/184741.pdf.

119   "False Memory Syndrome Foundation Newsletter," December 1997 - Vol. 6, No. 11, Newsletter Archives, False Memory Syndrome Foundation. http://www.fmsonline.org/newsletters/fmsf_1997_dec_v6_n11.pdf.

120   Mothers faced another barrier established by child molesters and their experts—parental alienation syndrome (PAS). Mothers supposedly alienated the father by convincing their child the father had molested them.

121   "FMS Foundation Newsletter," January 1, 1995 - Vol. 4, No. 1, Newsletter Archives, False Memory Syndrome Foundation. http://www.fmsonline.org/newsletters/fmsf_1995_jan_v4_n1.pdf.

122   "FMS Foundation Newsletter," March 15, 1992 - Vol. 1, No. 1, Newsletter Archives, False Memory Syndrome Foundation. http://www.fmsonline.org/newsletters/fmsf_1992_mar_v1_n1.pdf.

123   "FMS Foundation Newsletter," June 12, 1992 - Vol. 1, No. 6, Newsletter Archives, False Memory Syndrome Foundation. http://www.fmsonline.org/newsletters/fmsf_1992_june_v1_n6.pdf.

124   "FMS Foundation Newsletter," November 5, 1992 - Vol. 1, No. 10, Newsletter Archives, False Memory Syndrome Foundation. http://www.fmsonline.org/newsletters/fmsf_1992_nov_v1_n10.pdf.

125   Mike Stanton, "U-Turn on Memory Lane," *Colombia Journalism Review* 36, no. 2 (July/August 1997): 44. https://www.jimhopper.com/pdf/stanton1997.pdf.

126   "FMS Foundation Newsletter," December 7, 1993 - Vol. 2, No. 11, Newsletter Archives, False Memory Syndrome Foundation. http://www.fmsonline.org/newsletters/fmsf_1993_dec_v2_n11.pdf.

127   Orne reportedly received CIA funding through Project Subproject 84 in 1958.

128   J. P. Kahn, "Trial by Memory: Stung by Daughter's Claim of Abuse, a Writer Lashed Back," *The Boston Globe*, December 24, 1994. When asked in *Rodriguez v. Perez* if she had compared herself to Schindler, she responded, "That, that is absolutely false. It's been taken out of context and distorted."

129 Pierre Thomas, Jack Date, and Theresa Cook, "Captured: 'King of the Child Exploitation Suspects,'" ABC News, May 2, 2007. https://abcnews.go.com/TheLaw/story?id=3132195&page=1.

130 "Nightline #646722" ABC Special, starring Ted Koppel, Richard Berendzen, and Paul McHugh. Aired on May 23, 1990. Also includes Alan Kraut, Susan Allen, and Milton Greenberg. https://tvnews.vanderbilt.edu/broadcasts/646722.

131 David G. Savage, "Skeptics Dispute 'Recovered Memory' of Abuse: Despite Court Use of Technique, Some Psychiatrists Say Such Recollections Can't Be Blocked," *The Washington Post*, November 27, 1993, A-15.

132 McHugh at https://blogs.brown.edu/recoveredmemory/tag/paul-mchugh/

133 "Paidika Interview: Hollida Wakefield and Ralph Underwager Part I," Nudist Hall of Shame, No Status Quo. http://www.nostatusquo.com/ACLU/NudistHallofShame/.

134 Post to witchhnt@mitvma.edu, September 14, 1996.

135 "FMS Foundation Newsletter," March 1992.

136 "FMS Foundation Newsletter," April 1993.

137 "What Is Child Sexual Abuse?" Child Sexual Abuse, Violence Prevention, Centers for Disease Control and Prevention, last modified April 6, 2022. http://tiny.cc/t8zsuz

138 Based on $100/year membership dues.

139 "FMS Foundation Newsletter," January 1994.

140 Kahn, "Trial by Memory."

141 Judith Herman, "Presuming to Know the Truth," *Nieman Reports* (Spring 1994): 43.

142 Elizabeth F. Loftus and L. Cahill, "Memory Distortion: From Misinformation to Rich False Memory," *Foundations of Remembering* (2007): 413–425.

143 Ken Pope, "Open Letters to the APA Discrediting the FMS Foundation," 1995. http://astraeasweb.net/politics/fmsapa.html.

144 "FMS Foundation Newsletter," Nov/Dec 1995 - Vol. 4, No. 10, Newsletter Archives, False Memory Syndrome Foundation. http://www.fmsonline.org/newsletters/fmsf_1995_novdec_v4_n10.pdf.

145 David L. Calof, "A Conversation with Pamela Freyd, Ph.D. Co-Founder and Executive Director, False Memory Syndrome Foundation, Inc., Part I," *Treating Abuse Today* 3, no. 3: 25–33. http://www.clinicalworkshops.com/images/uploads/tat_pdfs/tat-interview-pamela-freyd.pdf.

146 However implausible or improbable, depictions of bestiality appear in prehistoric art.

147 Jonathan Bor, "One Family's Tragedy Spawns National Group," *Baltimore Sun*, December 9, 1994. https://www.baltimoresun.com/news/bs-xpm-1994-12-09-1994343022-story.html.

148 Mitchell, "Memories of a Disputed Past."

149 Katie Heaney, "The Memory War: Jennifer Freyd Accused Her Father of Sexual Abuse. Her Parents' Attempt to Discredit Her Created a Defense for Countless Sex Offenders," *The Cut*, January 6, 2021. https://www.thecut.com/article/false-memory-syndrome-controversy.html.

150 Jennifer Freyd, "Theoretical and Personal Perspectives on the Delayed Memory Debate," a presentation at the Center for Mental Health at Foote Hospital's Continuing Education Conference "Controversies Around Recovered Memories of Incest and Ritual Abuse," Ann Arbor, Michigan, August 7, 1993.

151 "FMS Foundation Newsletter," August 1993.

152 "Bill Cosby and the FMSF, Redux"; Recovered Memory Project: Case Archive, Commentary, and Scholarly Resources; June 17, 2017. https://blogs.brown.edu/recoveredmemory/tag/pamela-freyd/.

153 Indicators included (1) custody dispute, (2) neighborhood dispute, (3) history of conflict between the referral source and the alleged perpetrator, (4) history of multiple referrals that are consistently unfounded, (5) anonymous referral, (6) alleged perpetrators claim that the allegations are false, (7) undertones of retaliation or revenge, (8) the victim's statement is inconsistent with the developmental or age level, (9) indications that the child's statements were coached, (10) domestic violence, (11) intrafamilial or extended family conflict, (12) lack of medical or physical evidence, (13) the allegations lack specifics or details, and (14) the referral source lacks first-hand knowledge.

154 January Adams, "From Library Journal," Editorial Reviews, *Confabulations: Creating False Memories, Destroying Families*, Amazon. https://www.amazon.com/Confabulations-Creating-Memories-Destroying-Families/dp/0897771443.

155 Linda McEwen, email to author, May 2020. McEwen assisted on research for this book.

156 Family videos in Sasha Joseph Neulinger's 2020 documentary, *Rewind*, show a boy who is angry about the abuse and terrified of telling his parents that he is being raped by three adult male family members. His father films his behavior, his mother tries to understand his behavior, and viewers observe his behavior and are aware of the cause.

157 "FMS Foundation Newsletter," July/August 17, 1998 - Vol. 7, No. 6, Newsletter Archives, False Memory Syndrome Founda-

tion. http://www.fmsfonline.org/newsletters/fmsf_1998_julaug_v7_n6.pdf.

158   Joan C. Golston, "A False Memory Syndrome Conference Activist, Accused, and Their Professional Allies Talk about Science, Law and Family Reconciliation," *Treating Abuse Today* 5, no. 1 (January/February 1995): 24–30. http://www.clinicalworkshops.com/store/digital/details/vol_5_no_1.

159   Quoted in Bertram Karon and Anmarie Widener, "Repressed Memories: The Real Story," *Professional Psychology* 29, no. 5 (1998): 485.

160   Mary Knight, *Am I Crazy?*

161   Anna Salter, *Predators, Pedophiles, Rapists, and Other Sex Offenders* (New York: Basic Books, 2003): 57.

162   "Paidika Interview."

163   Richard A. Gardner, *Child Custody Litigation: A Guide for Parents and Mental Health Professionals* (Fresno: Creative Therapeutics, 1986): 93.

164   "FMS Foundation Newsletter," June 1992.

165   "FMS Foundation Newsletter," January 1994.

166   https://www.cdc.gov/violenceprevention/aces/about.html

167   Ives Cavalcante Passos et al., "Inflammatory Markers in Post-Traumatic Stress Disorder: A Systematic Review, Meta-Analysis, and Meta-Regression," *The Lancet.* 2, no. 11 (November 2015): 1002–1012.

168   https://www.ncbi.nlm.nih.gov/pmc/articles/PMC6289633/

CHAPTER 12

169   Khadija Rouf and Danny Taggart, "Do No Harm?" in *Trauma and Memory: The Science and the Silenced*, eds. Valerie Sinason and Ashley Conway (Oxford: Routledge 2021).

170   Thanks to Naomi Oreskes and Erik M. Conway for their detailed description in *Merchants of Doubt* of the tobacco industry's actions to obscure the dangers of smoking.

171   Daniel Goleman, "Childhood Trauma: Memory or Invention?" *The New York Times*, July 21, 1992, C-1. https://www.nytimes.com/1992/07/21/science/childhood-trauma-memory-or-invention.html.

172   Bill Dietrich, "UW Expert Challenges 'Repressed' Memories—Says Some Sexual Abuse May Not Be Real," *The Seattle Times*, August 13, 1992. https://archive.seattletimes.com/archive/?date=19920813&slug=1507215.

173   Elizabeth F. Loftus, "The Reality of Repressed Memories," a speech presented at annual APA conference, August 14–18, 1992 (cassette recording No. 92-220).

174 Hasher, L., Goldstein, D., & Toppino, T. (1977). Frequency and the Conference of Referential Validity. *Journal of Verbal Learning and Verbal Behavior*, 16, 107-112. http://bear.warrington.ufl.edu/brenner/mar7588/Papers/hasher-et-al-jvvb-1977.

175 Steven Elbow, "Crime and Courts: Rethinking the 'False Memory' Controversy," *The Cap Times*, April 17, 2011. https://madison.com/ct/news/local/crime_and_courts/blog/article_868cd71e-66ae-11e0-a171-001cc4c03286.html.

176 Ross E. Cheit, Yael Shavit, and Zachary Reiss-Davis, "Media Issues: Magazine Coverage of Child Sexual Abuse, 1992–2004," *Journal of Child Sexual Abuse* 19 (2010): 999–117. https://www.d.umn.edu/~jmaahs/Crime%20and%20Media/pdf%20files/Summer%202012/magazine%20coverage%20of%20child%20sex%20abuse.pdf.

177 Spelling the word as "lede" helped copyeditors, typesetters, and others in the business distinguish it from "lead," which referred to the thin strip of metal separating lines of type (as in a Linotype machine).

178 Stephen J. Flusberg et al., "Who's the 'Real' Victim? How Victim Framing Shapes Attitudes Toward Sexual Assault," *Psychological Science*, March 25, 2022. https://doi.org/10.1177/09567976211045935.

179 Colin Blakemore, "The Unsolved Marvel of Memory," *The New York Times*, February 6, 1977, SM42. https://www.nytimes.com/1977/02/06/archives/the-unsolved-marvel-of-memory-why-do-some-people-forget-what-they.html.

180 "Persuasive Techniques," Resources, Saylor.org Academy. https://resources.saylor.org/wwwresources/archived/site/wp-content/uploads/2014/01/K12ELA7-7.2.2-PersuasiveTechniquesHandout-BY-SA1.pdf.

181 Ellen Bass and Laura Davis, *The Courage to Heal: A Guide for Women Survivors of Child Sexual Abuse* (New York: Harper and Row). 251 buyers rated the book as 4.4 of 5 stars at Amazon.com in 2019.

182 The sentence was revised in a 1994 edition to read "If you genuinely think you were abused and your life shows the symptoms, there is a strong likelihood that you were."

183 Steve Novella, in "A Scientific Guide to Critical Thinking Skills" for *The Great Courses*, credited *The Courage to Heal* with creating "an epidemic of what is now known as false memory syndrome" (p. 33). To date, there is no evidence to support this claim.

184 Barbara Graham, "Swept Out of My Childhood into a Nameless Sea," Purple Clover, March 4, 2015. https://purpleclover.littleth-

ings.com/relationships/2316-swept-out-my-childhood-into-name-less-sea/.

185   "FMS Foundation Newsletter," January 1993.

186   Carol Tavris, "Beware the Incest-Survivor Machine," *The New York Times*, January 3, 1993, 7-1. http://www.nytimes.com/1993/01/03/books/beware-the-incest-survivor-machine.html?pagewanted=all.

187   "Real Incest and Real Survivors: Readers Respond," *The New York Times*, February 14, 1993.

188   "FMS Foundation Newsletter," October 5, 1992 - Vol. 1, No. 9, Newsletter Archives, False Memory Foundation Syndrome. http://www.fmsonline.org/newsletters/fmsf_1992_oct_v1_n9.pdf.

189   Locations mentioned in these anecdotal accounts were reported to the author.

190   Mitchell, "Memories of a Disputed Past."

191   "FMS Foundation Newsletter," January 1995.

192   "FMS Foundation Newsletter," May 3, 1993 - Vol. 2, No. 5, Newsletter Archives, False Memory Syndrome Foundation. http://www.fmsonline.org/newsletters/fmsf_1993_may_v2_n5.pdf.

193   Leon Jaroff, "Repressed-Memory Therapy: Lies of the Mind," *TIME*, November 29, 1993. http://content.time.com/time/subscriber/article/0,33009,979691-8,00.html.

194   Miriam Horn, "Memories Lost and Found," *U.S. News and World Report*, November 28, 1993, 52–63.

195   Mike Field, "False Memory Wreaks Havoc for Accused," *The Johns Hopkins University Gazette*, December 5, 1994. https://pages.jh.edu/gazette/1994/dec0594/memory.html.

196   "FMS Foundation Newsletter," May 1993.

197   "FMS Foundation Newsletter," November 1992.

198   Judith Herman, "Presuming to Know the Truth," *Nieman Report* 48 (1994): 43–45.

199   Sharon Begley, "You Must Remember This," *Newsweek*, September 25, 1994. https://www.newsweek.com/you-must-remember-188402.

CHAPTER 13

200   Lori Leigh Kondora, "A Textual Analysis of the Construction of the False Memory Syndrome: Representations in Popular Magazines, 1990–1995," The University of Washington, Madison ProQuest Dissertations Publishing (1997). https://www.proquest.com/docview/304382850/abstract/87ADE21F72F24808PQ/1?accountid=175359#.

201   Stephanie Salter, "A World I Never Knew," *The San Francisco Examiner*, April 1993.

202 Salter, "A World I Never Knew," A-19.

203 Stephanie Salter, "Feminist Treason and Intellectual Fascism," *The San Francisco Examiner*, April 7, 1993. https://www.trans-formation.dk/www.raven1.net/mcf/mindnet/mn122.htm.

204 Kerry Lauerman, "KRON Panel Coverage Criticized," *Forbes ASAP*, March 1994.

205 K. Brooks, "Casting Doubt: Memory Expert Elizabeth Loftus Tells Judges and Juries that Eyewitnesses May Not Recall the Whole Truth and Nothing but the Truth," *Pacific, The Seattle Times*, July 7, 1985.

206 Sandra G. Boodman, "At 28, Kathy O'Connor of Arlington Says She Remembered that Her Father Raped Her. She Sued Him and Lost. Are Delayed Memories Like Hers True or False?" *The Washington Post*, April 12, 1994. https://www.washingtonpost.com/archive/lifestyle/wellness/1994/04/12/at-28-kathy-oconnor-of-arlington-says-she-remembered-that-her-father-raped-her-she-sued-him-and-lost-are-delayed-memories-like-hers-true-or-false-/3909094b-6bfe-48d1-8f4e-893de8f86e99/.

207 Jeanne Supin, "The Long Shadow: Bruce Perry on the Lingering Effects of Childhood Trauma," *The Sun*, November 2016. https://www.thesunmagazine.org/issues/491/the-long-shadow.

208 Fred Bahson, "The World We Still Have: Barry Lopez on Restoring Our Lost Intimacy with Nature," *The Sun*, December 2019. https://www.thesunmagazine.org/issues/528/the-world-we-still-have.

209 http://tinyurl.com/jdcgx5c

210 Kathy Pezdek, Kimberly Finger, and Danelle Hodge, "Planting False Childhood Memories: The Role of Event Plausibility," *Psychological Science* 8, no. 6 (November 1997): 437–441. https://www.jstor.org/stable/40063230.

211 Murphy et al at https://slidelegend.com/lost-in-the-mall-wendy-murphy_59d72e4f1723dd5d0993b2aa.html

212 Bernice Andrews and Chris R. Brewin, "False Memories and Free Speech: Is Scientific Debate Being Suppressed?" *Applied Cognitive Psychology* 31, no. 1 (January/February 2017): 45–49. https://doi.org/10.1002/acp.3285.

213 Crook and McEwen, "Deconstructing the Lost in the Mall Study." https://www.tandfonline.com/doi/full/10.1080/15379418.2019.1601603

214 Blizard and Shaw, "False Memory or False Defense?"

215 https://blogs.brown.edu/recoveredmemory/files/2015/05/Loftus_Pickrell_PA_95.pdf

CHAPTER 14

216 Elizabeth F. Loftus, "How Reliable Is Your Memory?" *TED*, June 2013. https://www.ted.com/talks/elizabeth_loftus_how_reliable_is_your_memory?language=en.

217 Elizabeth F. Loftus, Julie Feldman, and Richard Dashiell, "The Reality of Illusory Memories," in *Memory Distortions: How Minds, Brains, and Societies Reconstruct the Past*, ed. D. L. Schacter (Cambridge: Harvard University Press, 1995): 47–68. http://psycnet.apa.org/record/1996-97286-001.

218 Crook and McEwen, "Deconstructing the Lost in the Mall Study."

219 Blizard and Shaw, "False Memory or False Defense?"

220 Marta Serra-Garcia and Uri Gneezy, "Nonreplicable Publications Are Cited More than Replicable Ones," *Science Advances* 7, no. 21 (May 21, 2021). https://advances.sciencemag.org/content/7/21/eabd1705.

221 Gowri Gopalakrishna et al., "Prevalence of Questionable Research Practices, Research Misconduct and Their Potential Explanatory Factors: A Survey among Academic Researchers in The Netherlands," *PLoS ONE* 17, no. 2 (February 16, 2022). https://doi.org/10.1371/journal.pone.0263023.

222 Anthony G. Greenwald, "What (and Where) Is the Ethical Code Concerning Researcher Conflict of Interest?" *Perspectives on Psychological Science* 4, no. 1 (2009), The Association for Psychological Science. https://faculty.washington.edu/agg/pdf/Gwald.ConflictOfInterest.PPS.2009.pdf.

223 Elizabeth F. Loftus and Terrence E. Burns, "Mental Shock Can Produce Retrograde Amnesia," *Memory & Cognition* 10, no. 4 (July 1982): 318–323. https://doi.org/10.3758/BF03202423.

224 Mary Koss, Shannon Tromp, and Melinda Tharan, "Traumatic Memories: Empirical Foundations, Forensic and Clinical Implications," *Clinical Psychology: Science and Practice* 2, no. 2 (June 1995): 120. https://doi.org/10.1111/j.1468-2850.1995.tb00034.x.

225 "In the Libby Case, A Grilling to Remember," Letter from the Courtroom, The Fed Page, Politics, *The Washington Post*, October 27, 2006. https://www.washingtonpost.com/wp-dyn/content/article/2006/10/26/AR2006102601612.html.

226 Richard S. Schmechel et al., "Beyond the Ken? Testing Jurors' Understanding of Eyewitness Reliability Evidence," *Jurimetrics* 46, no. 2 (Winter 2006): 177–214. https://www.jstor.org/stable/29762929.

227 Loftus, E.F. (1986). Experimental psychologist as advocate or impartial educator. *Law and Human Behavior*, 10, 63-78.

228 Rene Cantu, "In Fraud We Trust: Top 5 Cases of Misconduct in University Research," University Research Explained. https://research.uh.edu/the-big-idea/university-research-explained/five-cases-of-research-fraud/.

229 "Research Misconduct Policy," Executive Order No. 61, Executive Orders, PO Home, Policy Directory, University of Washington. https://www.washington.edu/admin/rules/policies/PO/EO61.html.

230 Crook and McEwen, "Deconstructing the Lost in the Mall Study."

231 Blizard and Shaw, "False Memory or False Defense?"

232 Loftus's website (http://staff.washington.edu/eloftus/) was examined on March 31, 2022.

233 Nicholas B. Diamond, Michael J. Armson, and Brian Levine, "The Truth Is Out There: Accuracy in Recall of Verifiable Real-World Events," *Psychological Science* 31, no. 12 (November 23, 2020): 1,544–1,556. https://doi.org/10.1177/0956797620954812.

CHAPTER 15

234 *Ramona v. Superior Court*, no. B111565, the Second District, Division One of the Superior Court of Los Angeles, August 19, 1997. https://law.justia.com/cases/california/court-of-appeal/4th/57/107.html.

235 Katy Butler, "Mixed Messages," *Los Angeles Times*, June 26, 1994. https://latimes.newspapers.com/search/?query=false%20memories%20katy%20butler&ymd=1994-06-26.

236 Shawna Ramona, "Letters to Book Review," *SFGate*, August 3, 1997. https://www.sfgate.com/books/article/LETTERS-TO-BOOK-REVIEW-2831685.php.

237 Goldston, "A False Memory Syndrome Conference."

238 Joan C. Golston, "Current Topics in Law and Mental Health: False Memory Syndrome, Multiple Personality and Ritual Sexual Abuse; The Growing Controversy," *Treating Abuse Today* 5, no. 1 (January/February 1995).

239 An informative account of the impact of false memory lawsuits on therapists can be found on pp. 56–57 of *A Sinister Subtraction* by psychiatrist Richard P. Kluft.

240 I heard the following anecdotal accounts from sources who asked not to be named: A Canadian client told her therapist that an article discussing suing therapists had mysteriously appeared on her bed while she was hospitalized. An Australian public television station aired *Frontline*'s "The Search for Satan." At the conclusion, the spokesperson mentioned a recently filed lawsuit against therapists and provided a phone number for the local FMS

group. Some survivors have said they received articles discussing settlement awards either anonymously or from family members. Some report receiving anonymous mailings that included a crude drawing depicting named therapists in a waste disposal site.

241 Alan W. Sheflin and Daniel Brown, "The False Litigant Syndrome: "Nobody Would Say That Unless It Was the Truth," *The Journal of Psychiatry & Law* 27, no. 4 (September 1999). https://doi.org/10.1177/009318539902700310.

242 "Deposition of Laura Pasley in the matter of *Laura Pasley and Jennifer Pasley, et al. vs. Michael Bruce Moore, MS et al.*," no.91-15047-F in the court of Texas, Dallas County, September 21 and October 2, 1992.

243 Glenna Whitely, "The Seduction of Gloria Grady," *D Magazine*, October 1, 1991. https://www.dmagazine.com/publications/d-magazine/1991/october/the-seduction-of-gloria-grady/.

244 "FMS Foundation Newsletter," Nov/Dec 2002 - Vol. 11, No. 6, Newsletter Archives, False Memory Syndrome Foundation. http://www.fmsfonline.org/newsletters/fmsf_2002_novdec_v11_n6.pdf.

245 I was in the Houston courtroom for three weeks in September and October 1997.

246 I interviewed Braun by telephone, July 17, 2016.

247 Settlement information provided by Braun's later attorney, Howard Brinton.

248 Personal communication with staff person on October 19, 1999.

249 Thomas Glasgow, *Complainant No. 1988-10343-01 v. Bennett G. Braun, MD*, State of Illinois Department of Professional Regulation. http://www.fmsfonline.org/links/usavpeterson-illinois-vbraun.html.

250 Braun's comment via email to author, April 1, 2022.

251 Lisa Donovan and Tribune Staff Writer, "Controversial Psychiatrist Suspended," *Chicago Tribune*, October 8, 1999. https://www.chicagotribune.com/news/ct-xpm-1999-10-08-9910080262-story.html.

252 Cynthia Hanson, "Dangerous Therapy: The Story of Patricia Burgus and Multiple Personality Disorder," *Chicago*, June 1, 1999. https://www.chicagomag.com/Chicago-Magazine/June-1998/Dangerous-Therapy-The-Story-of-Patricia-Burgus-and-Multiple-Personality-Disorder/.

253 Susan Dunlap, "Butte Psychiatrist with Troubled Past Faces New Suit Alleging Negligence," *Montana Standard*, May 5, 2019. https://mtstandard.com/news/local/butte-psychiatrist-with-troubled-past-faces-new-suit-alleging-negligence/article_e5ea7374-cf9f-5176-be37-1ad72d8be5bc.html.

CHAPTER 16

254 Stanton, "U-Turn on Memory Lane."

255 Laura S. Brown, "Sacred Space, not Sacred Cows, or It's Never Fun Being Prophetic," *American Psychologist* 53, no. 4 (April 1998): 488–490. https://web.p.ebscohost.com/ehost/detail/detail?vid=0&sid=412222ad-0f70-45fd-b4b8-2ee88f6b4ca7%40redis&bdata=JnNpdGU9ZWhvc3Qtb-Gl2ZQ%3d%3d#AN=1998-00766-034&db=pdh.

256 Anna C. Salter, "Confessions of a Whistle-Blower: Lessons Learned," *Ethics & Behavior* 8, no. 2 (January 8, 2010): 115–124. https://doi.org/10.1207/s15327019eb0802_2.

257 "Surviving a Legacy of Incest," *The Institute Notebook* 1, no. 1 (Winter 1992), Pennsylvania Hospital. https://evegwrites.files.wordpress.com/2011/09/the-institute-notebook.pdf.

258 "FMS Foundation Newsletter," November 1993.

259 Quina, K. (1994a, Winter). Editorial. Psychology of Women Newsletter, 12-13. See also:
Quina, K. (1994b, Summer). Delayed memories or goat guts? [Letter to the editor]. Psychology of Women Newsletter, 6-9.

260 Lynne Henderson, "Suppressing Memory," *Law & Social Inquiry* 22, no. 3 (July 28, 2006): 695–732. https://doi.org/10.1111/j.1747-4469.1997.tb01085.x.

261 Michele Landsberg, "False Memory Label Invented by Lobby Group," *Toronto Star*, November 13, 1993. https://casac.ca/false-memory-label-invented-by-lobby-group/.

262 D. Seller, "News Story Missed the Mark," *Toronto Star*, May 27, 1995, B-2.

263 Ross Cheit, "Faux First Amendment Advocate, Debbie Nathan," The Witch-Hunt Narrative, April 28, 2016. https://blogs.brown.edu/rcheit/tag/debbie-nathan/.

264 Nathan at *"The Village Voice,"* September 29, 1987, 19–23, 26–32.

265 "From The Washington Post," Editorial Reviews, Making Monsters: False Memories, Psychotherapy, And Sexual Hysteria, Amazon. https://www.amazon.com/dp/0520205839?ie=UTF8&*entries*=0&viewID=&*Version*=1.

266 Katy Butler, "Did Daddy Really Do It?" Articles, *Katy Butler*, February 5, 2005. http://www.katybutler.com/author/articles/did-daddy-really-do-it/.

267 I emailed Williams, noting his thought-provoking review of *Capturing the Friedmans*. In turn, he described the backchannel responses he'd received and forwarded the emails.

268 S. Simone, "Journal Note," From Gallows Hill, Salem Massachusetts, *International Newspaper of the International Transactional Analysis Association*, January 14, 1997.

269 Cases must be referred to the Landelijk Expertise Bureau Bijzondere Zedenzaken (LEBZ) in the Netherlands if they contain ritual elements, recovered memories, or sexual abuse of a child before the age of three. The LEBZ serves as a de facto graveyard for such cases—they are rarely examined.

270 Sanne Terlingen, Huub Jaspers, and Sophie Blok, "Shards of Glass and Dark Rituals," *Argos*, 2020. https://www.vpro.nl/argos/lees/nieuws/2020/glass-shards-and-dark-rituals-english-transcript-.html.

271 "Board Control No. 600 2016 000373," The California Board of Psychology.

CHAPTER 17

272 https://dynamic.uoregon.edu/jjf/suggestedrefs.html

273 Salter, "Confessions of a Whistle-Blower."

274 Salter, "Confessions of a Whistle-Blower."

275 Salter, "Confessions of a Whistle-Blower," 123.

276 *Inside the False Memory Movement* and *The False Memory Movement's Political Agenda* are available for purchase at http://www.clinicalworkshops.com/store/physical/details/vol_4_no_6.

277 The conference was called "Beyond Confrontation and Mistrust: The 1st Northwest Conference on Family Mediation for Families Torn by Allegations of Abuse."

278 Laura S. Brown, "The Prices of Resisting Silence: Comments on Calof, Cheit, Freyd, Hoult, and Salter," *Ethics and Behavior* 8, no. 2 (1998): 189–193. https://doi.org/10.1207/s15327019eb0802_6.

279 Ed Penhale, "Father Torn by Incest Accusation," *Seattle Post-Intelligencer*, December 11, 1992. http://www.stopbadtherapy.com/resource/article/noah.shtml.

280 The ACLU filed an amicus supporting position that there is no scientific evidence for the theory of repression (*New Hampshire v Hungerford* appeal, Feb 1997).

281 *State v. Noah*, no. 41241-8-I, 43049-3-I, Court of Appeals of Washington, Division 1, September 11, 2000. https://caselaw.findlaw.com/wa-court-of-appeals/1018053.html.

282 David Calof, "Notes from a Practice Under Siege: Harassment, Defamation, and Intimidation in the Name of Science," *Ethics & Behavior* 8, no. 2 (1998): 161–187. https://ritualabuse.us/research/memory-fms/notes-from-a-practice-under-siege/.

283 David L. Corwin and Erna Olafson, "Videotaped Discovery of a Reportedly Unrecallable Memory of Child Sexual Abuse: Com-

parison with a Childhood Interview Videotape 11 Years Before," *Child Maltreatment* 2, no. 2 (May 1, 1997): 91–112. https://doi.org/10.1177/1077559597002002001.

284 A University of Washington librarian asked database subscribers to run a search for Taus on a restricted database:

Newsgroups: gov.us.topic.info.libraries.govdocs
From: Cheryl Nyberg <cnyn...@u.washington.edu>
Date: 1997/09/05
Subject: Military City Database subscribers

For a faculty member here, I am continuing to look for a member of the armed forces named **Nicole Taus**. I have recently discovered a commercial database that provides searchable databases for active and retired military personnel, but the databases are restricted to subscribers.

If you or your library subscribe and would be willing to run a search for **Nicole Taus**, I would be grateful.

Please respond directly to me and not to the list.

Thanks in advance,

Cheryl Nyberg

Cheryl Rae Nyberg
Reference Librarian
Gallagher Law Library
University of Washington

285 Nicole's biological mother submitted a declaration in July 2007 describing her (by then) terminated relationship with Loftus. The declaration is online at http://www.leadershipcouncil.org/1/lg/taus.html.

286 *"Taus v. Loftus et al.: Why Is This Case Important?"* The Leadership Council on Child Abuse & Interpersonal Violence. http://www.leadershipcouncil.org/1/lg/taus.html.

287 Tsang interview at http://kuci.org/~dtsang/subversity/pr021112.htm

288 "FMS Foundation Newsletter," July/Aug 2001 - Vol. 10, No. 4, Newsletter Archives, False Memory Syndrome Foundation. http://www.fmsonline.org/newsletters/fmsf_2001_julyaug_v10_n4.pdf.

289 Christopher Shea, "The Next Memory War," *The Boston Globe*, December 7, 2003. http://archive.boston.com/news/globe/ideas/articles/2003/12/07/the_next_memory_war/.

290 "Order Denying Plaintiff's Motion to Quash Defendant City of Wenatchee Subpoena for Records Deposition; Witness Loftus's

Motion to Quash Records Subpoena," *Manual Hidalgo Rodriguez vs. Robert Perez et al.*, No. CS-01-003-RHW, United States District Court Eastern District of Washington, September 12, 2003.

291 Elizabeth F. Loftus and Melvin J. Guyer, "Who Abused Jane Doe? The Hazards of the Single Case History: Part I," *Skeptical Inquirer* 26, no. 3 (2002): 24–32. https://staff.washington.edu/eloftus/Articles/JaneDoe.htm.

292 Amy Wilson, "War & Remembrance," *Orange County Register*, November 3, 2002. http://williamcalvin.com/2002/OrangeCtyRegister.htm.

293 Carol Tavris, "Whatever Happened to 'Jane Doe'? *Skeptical Inquirer* 32, no. 1 (January/February 2008). https://skepticalinquirer.org/2008/01/whatever-happened-to-jane-doe/.

294 "Supreme Court Decision," *Nicole Taus* v. *Elizabeth Loftus*, no. FCS021557, Superior Court of California, Solano County, February 26, 2007: 26. http://www.leadershipcouncil.org/docs/CASupCt.pdf.

295 "Supreme Court Decision."

296 "Declaration of Joan Blackwell in Support of Plaintiff Nicole Taus's Opposition to Defendants' Motion for Award of Fees," *Nicole Taus v. Elizabeth Loftus et al.*, No. FCS021557, Superior Court of the State of California, County of Solano. http://leadershipcouncil.org/docs/Declaration%20of%20Joan%20Blackwell%20final.pdf.

297 Elizabeth F. Loftus, "The Fiction of Memory," *TED*, June 11, 2013. https://www.ted.com/talks/elizabeth_loftus_how_reliable_is_your_memory/transcript?language=en.

298 "FMS Foundation Newsletter," October 1993.

299 Pamela Freyd's email to media outlets, September 7, 1998. http://smokyhole.org/sdhok/fmsf.htm.

300 Mark Smith, "Former Patient Can't Attribute False Memories to Therapy," *Houston Chronicle*, October 9, 1998.

301 "Judge Dismissed Case against Judith Peterson et al.," Abuse Recovery, Google Groups. https://groups.google.com/g/alt.abuse.recovery/c/aMc1kkiLAC8.

302 J. Thomas, "Federal Court Failed When It Tried to Criminalize Therapy, Psychologists Contents After Mistrial," *The National Psychologist*, May 1, 1999.

CHAPTER 18

303 Sylvia Solinski, "Knowing and Not Knowing, A Frequent Human Arrangement," *Journal of Trauma & Dissociation* 18, no. 3 (2017): 387–408. https://doi.org/10.1080/15299732.2017.1295423.

304 Paul Wilkes, "Unholy Acts," The New Yorker, May 30, 1993.

305 Victor I. Vieth, "Suffer the Children: Developing Effective Church Policies on Child Maltreatment," *Jacob's Hope: A Newsletter of the Jacob Wetterling Resource Center*," June 2011.

306 Warwick Middleton, "A Life Sentence: How the Study of Ongoing Incest During Adulthood Informs about the Nature of Organized Abuse," Webinar, International Society for the Study of Trauma and Dissociation, October 13, 2018.

307 Pope Benedict XVI, "Pope's Child Porn 'Normal' Claim Sparks Outrage Among Victims," *Belfast Telegraph*, December 21, 2012. https://www.belfasttelegraph.co.uk/news/world-news/popes-child-porn-normal-claim-sparks-outrage-among-victims-28577483.html.

308 Deposed for the defense in *Liano v. The Phoenix Diocese*, Loftus named the accused priests she had testified for. "Well, I did some work for the Boston diocese, the Spokane diocese, the Portland diocese . . . Yes, Cardinal Law . . . Well, Father Shanley was one of them, and then there was Bernardin from Chicago (p. 36)."

309 A court employee reported that Shanley's niece paid $15,000 for Loftus's testimony, which included door to door travel time.

310 "February 4, 2005: Analysis of Loftus' Testimony," *Paul Shanley Trial Blog*, The Leadership Council on Child Abuse & Interpersonal Violence. http://www.leadershipcouncil.org/1/blog/s.html.

311 Dahlia Lithwick, "Slate's Jurisprudence: Repressed Memories and the Courts," NPR, February 8, 2005. https://www.npr.org/2005/02/08/4490707/slates-jurisprudence-repressed-memories-and-the-courts.

312 "February 15, 2005: Responding to Misinformation in the Media," *Paul Shanley Trial Blog*, The Leadership Council on Child Abuse & Interpersonal Violence. http://www.leadershipcouncil.org/1/blog/s.html.

313 Jonathan Rauch, "If Paul Shanley Is a Monster, the State Didn't Prove It," *The Atlantic*, March 2005. https://www.theatlantic.com/magazine/archive/2005/03/if-paul-shanley-is-a-monster-the-state-didnt-prove-it/303873/.

314 Joann Wypijewski, "Oscar Hangover Special: Why 'Spotlight' Is a Terrible Film," *Counterpunch*, February 29, 2016. https://www.counterpunch.org/2016/02/29/oscar-hangover-special-why-spotlight-is-a-terrible-film/.

315 Maureen Orth, "Unholy Communion," *Vanity Fair*, August 2002. https://www.vanityfair.com/news/2002/08/orth200208.

316 "Brief of Amicus Curiae: False Memory Syndrome Foundation," *Commonwealth v. Paul R. Shanley*, no. SJC-10382, Commonwealth of Massachusetts Supreme Judicial Court, Middlesex

County. http://www.fmsfonline.org/links/fmsfamicusshanley.html.

317 "Brief of the Leadership Council as Amicus Curiae," *Commonwealth of Massachusetts v. Paul Shanley*, no. 10382, Commonwealth of Massachusetts Supreme Judicial Court. http://leadershipcouncil.org/docs/ShanleyBrief.pdf.

318 *The Associated Press*, "Abusive Ex-Priest Shanley Release from Prison, to Live in Ware," *Telegram & Gazette*, published July 28, 2017, last updated July 29, 2017. https://www.telegram.com/story/news/local/south-west/2017/07/28/ex-priest-shanley-to-live-across-street-from-ware-dance-studio/20050357007/.

319 Survey data available on request from the author.

320 Many of those who reported may have been silenced with, "Your memories are false."{

321 Mike Baker, "'Deep Regret' Inside Portland-Based Mercy Corps As Aid Organization Grapples with Sexual Abuse," *The Seattle Times*, published May 19, 2021, updated May 20, 2021. https://www.seattletimes.com/nation-world/deep-regret-inside-aid-organization-grappling-with-sexual-abuse/?utm_source=marketingcloud&utm_medium=email&utm_campaign=Morning+Brief+5-20-21_5_20_2021&utm_term=Active%20subscriber.

322 T. C. Kelly, "Bill Cosby Uses Memory Expert to Challenge Accusers," *ExpertPages Blog*, December 6, 2016. https://blog.expertpages.com/expertwitness/bill-cosby-uses-memory-expert-to-challenge-accusers.htm.

323 Bill Lyon, "Who Is Jerry Sandusky," *The Philadelphia Inquirer*, November 5, 2011. https://www.inquirer.com/philly/sports/colleges/20111106_Bill_Lyon__Who_is_Jerry_Sandusky_.html.

324 "Appeal from the PCRA Order Entered October 18, 2017, in the Court of Common Pleas of Centre County Criminal Division," no. 1654 MDA 2017, *Commonwealth of Pennsylvania v. Gerald A. Sandusky*, Superior Court of Pennsylvania, February 5, 2019. https://www.courtlistener.com/opinion/4587530/com-v-sandusky-g/.

325 Paulina Dedaj, "Simone Biles Details How Nassar's Abuse Impacted Tokyo Olympics: 'I Never Should Have Been Left Alone,'" Fox News, September 15, 2021. https://www.foxnews.com/sports/simone-biles-nassar-abuse-impacted-tokyo-olympics-left-alone.

326 Christina Carrega, Evan Perez, and Devan Cole, "Justice Department Watchdog Blasts FBI's Handling of Allegations against Larry Nassar," CNN, July 14, 2021. https://www.cnn.com/2021/07/14/politics/larry-nassar-fbi-justice-department-review/index.html.

327 "Unknown: What Happened in the Attic; Known: Memory Is Malleable," *The National Law Journal*, February 24, 2014. https://www.law.com/nationallawjournal/almID/1202644116038/unknown-what-happened-in-the-attic-known-memory-is-malleable/.

328 Adam Klasfeld, "'False Memory' Expert Involved in Robert Durst, O. J. Simpson, and Harvey Weinstein Cases Testifies for Ghislaine Maxwell," *Law & Crime*, December 16, 2021. https://lawandcrime.com/live-trials/ghislaine-maxwell/false-memory-expert-involved-in-robert-durst-o-j-simpson-and-harvey-weinstein-cases-testifies-for-ghislaine-maxwell/.

329 Amanda Darrach, "'I Want to Go to the Ghislaine Maxwell Trial," *Colombia Journalism Review*, December 22, 2021. https://www.cjr.org/special_report/ghislaine-maxwell-epstein-trial.php.

330 John Sweeny, "Miss Sweden and Bugs Bunny Add Up to a Bad Day in Court for Ghislaine Maxwell," *The Guardian*, December 18, 2021. https://www.theguardian.com/us-news/2021/dec/18/miss-sweden-and-bugs-bunny-add-up-to-a-bad-day-in-court-for-ghislaine-maxwell?CMP=Share_iOSApp_Other.

CHAPTER 20

331 Signe Wilkinson, "Dr. Vic Timm," *The Anchor*, December 10, 1993, 3. https://issuu.com/the_anchor/docs/12.10.93.

332 "Bishop Apologizes for Cartoon Lampooning Priest Sex Abuse Victims," *AP News*, December 15, 1993. https://apnews.com/article/1b36dbe79b0eed05f276d7fdea5ea59e.

333 "Report on Memories of Childhood Abuse: American Medical Association Council of Scientific Affairs," *International Journal of Clinical and Experimental Hypnosis* 43, no. 2 (1995): 114–117. https://doi.org/10.1080/00207149508409955.

334 Eva Doehr, "Inside the False Memory Movement," *Treating Abuse Today* 4, no. 6 (1994).

335 Lynn Schirmer, "Creative Cooking," *Treating Abuse Today* (May/June 1997).

336 *Fatal Memories*, directed by Daryl Duke, written by Audrey Davis Lenin, featuring Shelley Long et al., aired in 1992. https://www.imdb.com/title/tt0104236/.

337 "Divided Memories Part 1," *Frontline*, episode 12, produced by Ofra Bikel, aired in 1995 on PBS: https://www.pbs.org/wgbh/frontline/film/divided-memories-part-1/.

338 A character in Sue Grafton's *U is for Undertow* (2009) saw a therapist who insisted he was molested. Grafton's character sues his parents in 1981, seven years before the first state allowed such lawsuits.

339 Joel Mathis, "The Ugly Harassment of Sara Ganim," "City Life," *Philadelphia*, February 19, 2013. https://www.phillymag.com/news/2013/02/19/ugly-harassment-sara-ganim/#7shLP6eaxB7ctoQJ.99.

340 "The Salt Lake Tribune Staff," The 2017 Pulitzer Prize Winner in Local Reporting, The Pulitzer Prizes. https://www.pulitzer.org/winners/salt-lake-tribune-staff.

341 Elizabeth J. Letourneau and Tonya C. Lewis, "The Portrayal of Child Sexual Assault in Introductory Psychology Textbooks," *Teaching of Psychology* 26, no. 4 (October 1, 1999): 253–258. https://doi.org/10.1207/S15328023TOP260402.

342 Chris R. Brewin, Bernice Andrews, and Laura Mickes, "Regaining Consensus on the Reliability of Memory," *Current Directions in Psychological Science* 29, no. 2 (January 30, 2020): 121–125. https://doi.org/10.1177/0963721419898122.

343 Letourneau and Lewis, "The Portrayal of Child Sexual Assault."

344 Letourneau and Lewis, "The Portrayal of Child Sexual Assault."

345 Sarah Brookhart, "Shipping News: Increasing Public Understanding of Psychological Science," *Observer* 17, no. 12 (December 12, 2004). https://www.psychologicalscience.org/observer/shipping-news-increasing-public-understanding-of-psychological-science. Participants included Elliot Aronson, University of California, Santa Cruz; Sharon Begley, *The Wall Street Journal*; Ludy T. Benjamin, Jr., Texas A&M University; Robert Cialdini, Arizona State University; Peter Clarke, University of Southern California; K. C. Cole, *Los Angeles Times*; Alan Leshner, American Association for the Advancement of Science; Elizabeth F. Loftus, University of California, Irvine; Richard McNally, Harvard University; Joe Palca, *National Public Radio*; Jon Palfreman, Palfreman Film Group; Muriel Pearson, *ABC Primetime Live*; Elizabeth Ruksznis, *Dateline NBC*; Holly Stocking, Indiana University; Carol Tavris, Los Angeles, California. Alan G. Kraut, Sarah Brookhart, and Brian L. Weaver of APS also attended the meeting.

346 David H. Gleaves, "What Are Students Learning About Trauma, Memory, and Dissociation?" *Journal of Trauma & Dissociation* 8, no. 4 (October 12, 2008): 1–5. https://doi.org/10.1300/J229v08n04_01.

347 Jamie L. Kissee, Lahela J. Isaacson, and Cindy Miller-Perrin, "An Analysis of Child Maltreatment Content in Introductory Psychology Textbooks," *Journal of Aggression, Maltreatment & Trauma* 23, no. 3 (March 27, 2014): 215–228. https://doi.org/10.1080/10926771.2014.878891.

348 Bethany L. Brand and Linda E. McEwen, "Coverage of Childhood Maltreatment and Its Effects in Three Introductory Psy-

chology Textbooks," *Trauma Psychology News, Division 56 of the American Psychological Association* (Fall 2014): 8–11.

349 The trauma survey is online at https://psycnet.apa.org/search/display?id=4bd34ba4-9248-7090-1dd3-c6db999afb4&recordId=63&tab=PA&page=3&display=25&sort=Publication-YearMSSort%20desc,AuthorSort%20asc&sr=1

350 American Psychological Association, "Tea with TOPSS and Elizabeth Loftus, PhD (August 13, 2020)," YouTube. https://www.youtube.com/watch?v=FjD88UNtLWM.

CONCLUSION

351 https://www.routledge.com/Trauma-and-Memory-The-Science-and-the-Silenced/Sinason-Conway/p/book/9781032044293

352 https://eassurvey.wordpress.com/2022/03/31/journal-of-trauma-dissociation-the-science-and-politics-of-false-memories/

353 Alan W. Scheflin and Daniel Brown, "Repressed Memory or Dissociative Amnesia: What the Science Says," *Journal of Psychiatry & Law* 24, no. 2 (1996): 143–188. https://doi.org/10.1177/009318539602400203.

Appendix

UNIVERSITY OF WASHINGTON   6/9
HUMAN SUBJECTS DIVISION JM-22

Form HS SR-1 (rev 3/94)

STATUS REPORT: Application no. __23-332-C__

BOX FOR COMMITTEE	
MASTER ☒	COMMITTEE ☐
REVIEWER ☐	INVESTIGATOR ☐

__24-316-C__
APPLICATION NUMBER

CHECK AS APPROPRIATE:

☐ DO NOT RENEW. Complete items 1 - 6 of Status Report and return form.

☒ RENEW WITH MINOR OR NO CHANGES. Complete items 1 -10 of Status Report; submit four (4) copies of this form.

☐ RENEW WITH CHANGES IN PROCEDURES, POPULATION, OR PURPOSE. Complete and submit nine (9) copies of a new HSRC application (UW 13-11) and this Status Report (items 1.-10.).

1. Investigator's name, position, division and department, mail stop and telephone number:

E.F. Loftus, Professor, A&S, Psychology, NI-25, 53-7184

2. Title of Human Subjects Application:

Childhood Memories

3. Brief summary of findings to date (add sheets if necessary):

24 subjects have been run. About 8-9% have formed false positive memories. Another 10-15% formed partial false memories. The memories appear to be less clear and vivid than true memories.

4. Number and types of adverse effects and how they were handled (add sheets if necessary):

5. No. of subjects enrolled in study to date: __24__ Normals/Controls ____ Patients/Case

6. No. of subjects added during past year of approval: __24__ Normals/Controls ____ Patients/Case

7. No. of subjects continuing participation: __6__ Normals/Controls ____ Patients/Case

8. How many new subjects will join the study over the next year?   __20__ Normals/Controls ____ Patients/Case

9. Do you propose any minor changes in this study or consent form? ☒ No ☐ Yes   If yes, describe (add sheets if necessary). Submit 4 copies of revised consent form and other materials, if appropriate.

10. Provide information for all funding, awarded or proposed for this activity (add sheets if necessary).   no funding

   a. Type: ☐ research grant, ☐ contract, ☐ fellowship, ☐ training grant, ☐ other, explain:

   b. Name of principal investigator:

   c. Name of agency: Agency's no. (if assigned):

   d. Title of proposal:

   e. Inclusive dates: from _____, through _____

   f. Submitted through Grant and Contract Services? ☐ No ☐ Yes ☐ VAMC ☐ Other : _____

HSRC Chair's signature: _Edward Donnerstein_   Date : JUN 5 1994   Approve ☒ Disapprove ☐
Subject to the following conditions:
Period of approval is one year, from __08-10-94__   through __08-09-95__

* VALID ONLY AS LONG AS APPROVED PROCEDURES ARE FOLLOWED *

Child Maltreatment—Percentage of Cases Substantiated

Comparison with years prior to 2018 adjusted for new definition of victim (without alternative response)

Table 3–2	2020	2019	2018	2017	2016	2015
	%	%	%	%	%	%
Alabama	29.7%	27.8%	29.5%	26.3%	26.2%	26.3%
Alaska	17.2%	18.1%	18.2%	18.8%	24.7%	24.3%
Arizona	11.2%	13.4%	15.0%	10.1%	9.6%	12.9%
Arkansas	15.0%	13.0%	12.8%	13.7%	14.9%	14.3%
California	17.4%	16.4%	15.5%	15.6%	15.9%	16.8%
Colorado	23.8%	23.7%	23.7%	23.7%	23.5%	23.7%
Connecticut	42.0%	40.1%	35.7%	31.2%	31.9%	29.1%
Delaware	10.4%	9.0%	9.3%	10.3%	9.9%	9.4%
District of Columbia	16.6%	13.2%	10.5%	10.3%	9.6%	10.3%
Florida	9.7%	9.8%	10.7%	11.5%	12.5%	13.5%
Georgia	6.1%	5.3%	5.6%	5.1%	10.7%	14.0%
Hawaii	25.4%	29.4%	32.7%	35.8%	39.2%	40.2%
Idaho	12.5%	10.8%	11.9%	12.9%	13.4%	11.1%
Illinois	22.3%	19.2%	18.9%	19.1%	18.2%	21.6%
Indiana	12.7%	12.1%	12.3%	13.8%	15.3%	15.3%
Iowa	25.3%	25.3%	24.7%	25.2%	24.3%	23.5%
Kansas	6.4%	7.0%	9.6%	12.9%	7.2%	6.1%
Kentucky	22.5%	23.4%	25.1%	24.6%	24.8%	22.7%
Louisiana	27.6%	29.0%	34.3%	35.2%	31.4%	32.1%
Maine	20.6%	23.4%	28.2%	27.9%	26.5%	24.0%
Maryland	23.7%	23.2%	23.6%	22.8%	21.4%	21.4%
Massachusetts	33.3%	31.6%	31.1%	30.9%	37.5%	38.4%
Michigan	17.8%	16.9%	19.7%	21.0%	20.7%	19.7%
Minnesota	16.3%	15.6%	17.6%	19.3%	18.5%	15.4%
Mississippi	21.5%	21.0%	21.3%	23.1%	23.2%	22.4%
Missouri	6.0%	5.8%	5.4%	5.1%	5.7%	6.1%
Montana	20.7%	20.4%	21.0%	21.3%	18.9%	12.4%
Nebraska	7.7%	9.4%	9.3%	10.7%	10.3%	12.8%
Nevada	15.9%	15.3%	15.1%	15.4%	15.5%	15.3%
New Hampshire	7.5%	8.0%	8.1%	8.0%	5.4%	5.6%
New Jersey	4.6%	5.6%	6.8%	7.9%	9.8%	11.4%
New Mexico	23.9%	27.6%	27.9%	28.8%	29.1%	28.2%
New York	27.8%	28.7%	29.0%	30.0%	28.6%	29.8%
North Carolina	19.3%	5.0%	5.2%	5.4%	5.2%	5.6%

North Dakota	27.0%	25.4%	26.7%	27.5%	25.7%	25.7%
Ohio	20.7%	20.3%	20.6%	20.9%	20.5%	20.5%
Oklahoma	23.0%	24.1%	23.7%	23.8%	23.9%	22.8%
Oregon	21.3%	21.8%	22.5%	21.8%	20.0%	24.1%
Pennsylvania	13.3%	12.0%	10.8%	10.4%	10.5%	10.8%
Puerto Rico	29.1%	31.8%	29.3%	31.3%		25.5%
Rhode Island	31.2%	30.6%	30.0%	37.8%	35.7%	34.2%
South Carolina	19.4%	18.3%	19.5%	21.2%	23.0%	26.2%
South Dakota	36.2%	35.5%	36.1%	29.8%	28.3%	23.2%
Tennessee	8.8%	8.9%	9.0%	8.3%	8.8%	9.9%
Texas	22.9%	21.4%	20.7%	19.9%	19.6%	21.9%
Utah	34.0%	35.6%	35.1%	34.6%	34.5%	33.6%
Vermont	15.5%	17.9%	19.4%	17.6%	16.6%	16.4%
Virginia	11.5%	11.3%	11.4%	9.4%	8.8%	9.4%
Washington	7.5%	7.7%	8.7%	9.5%	10.4%	11.5%
West Virginia	11.9%	11.9%	12.6%	11.6%	11.2%	10.5%
Wisconsin	11.4%	11.4%	12.1%	12.1%	12.2%	11.5%
Wyoming	22.4%	18.8%	18.4%	15.5%	16.5%	14.7%
Overall	**17.5%**	**16.7%**	**16.9%**	**17.0%**	**17.3%**	**18.1%**

Substantiated Cases Over Time

U.S. Department of Health & Human Services, Administration for Children and Families, Administration on Children, Youth and Families, Children's Bureau. (2022).

Child Maltreatment 2020 (Table 3-2). Available from https://www.acf.hhs.gov/cb/data-research/child-maltreatment

Made in the USA
Las Vegas, NV
08 September 2022

54866210R10120